HERETICS!

The Wondrous (and Dangerous) Beginnings of Modern Philosophy

Steven Nadler
and Ben Nadler

Princeton University Press
Princeton and Oxford

Published by Princeton University Press,
41 William Street, Princeton, New Jersey 08540

In the United Kingdom: Princeton University Press,
6 Oxford Street, Woodstock, Oxfordshire OX20 1TR

press.princeton.edu

Jacket art by Ben Nadler

ISBN 978-0-691-16869-2

Library of Congress Cataloging-in-Publication Data
Names: Nadler, Steven M., 1958– author.
Title: Heretics! : the wondrous (and dangerous) beginnings of modern
philosophy / Steven Nadler and Ben Nadler.
Description: Princeton, NJ : Princeton University Press, 2017.
Identifiers: LCCN 2016034059 | ISBN 9780691168692 (pbk. : alk. paper)
Subject: LCSH: Philosophy, Modern—17th century.
Classification: LCC B801 .N335 2017 | DDC 190.9/032—dc23 LC record
available at https://lccn.loc.gov/2016034059

British Library Cataloging-in-Publication Data is available

This book has been composed in
Sabon Next LT Pro and a custom typeface

Printed on acid-free paper. ∞

Printed in China

1 3 5 7 9 10 8 6 4 2

Introduction

Something remarkable happened in the seventeenth century. It took place both on a grand cosmic scale and in the most intimate way. Philosophers in the 1600s pursued a new understanding of the universe and a new way of thinking about ourselves. Or perhaps it is more accurate to say the philosophers pursued new *ways* of thinking about these things, since they were not all in agreement on how the world works and what we are. They were at odds over what bodies are made of and what makes them move. They held disparate views about the existence of God and God's relationship to the world. They argued over what knowledge is and where it comes from. Many of the "new" thinkers believed that human beings are metaphysically and morally special and exempt from the laws that govern the rest of nature – we have souls and free will. Others insisted that, on the contrary, we are not some kind of "kingdom" unto ourselves; our bodies and our minds are as much a part of nature as anything else. Some even went so far as to say that we are nothing but matter in motion and thus no more free from determining causes than are rocks and trees.

Despite all these differences, this diverse and highly contentious group of philosophers shared some basic assumptions. They believed that the older, medieval approach to making sense of the world – with its spiritual forms and occult powers, its concern to defend Christian doctrine and its often uncritical devotion to the theories of Aristotle or Plato – no longer worked and needed to be replaced by more useful and intellectually independent models. They agreed that natural philosophy – what we now call "science" – should seek explanations of things grounded in the familiar, not the obscure. Above all, they insisted philosophy should proceed not by deference to what ancient authors had to say or what

RELIGIOUS AUTHORITIES DEMANDED, BUT FROM THE CLEAR AND DISTINCT IDEAS OF REASON AND THE EVIDENT TESTIMONY OF EXPERIENCE.

WHAT WAS THE MOST BRILLIANT CENTURY IN EUROPEAN HISTORY? COMPELLING ARGUMENTS COULD BE MADE ON BEHALF OF ATHENS IN THE FOURTH CENTURY BCE, WHERE SOCRATES, PLATO, AESCHYLUS, SOPHOCLES, AND ARISTOPHANES FLOURISHED UNDER PERICLEAN DEMOCRACY; THE TWELFTH CENTURY, WHICH SAW THE REDISCOVERY OF ARISTOTLE AND THE EMERGENCE OF UNIVERSITIES AND HIGH SCHOLASTIC THOUGHT; AND, OF COURSE, THE ITALIAN RENAISSANCE. AND YET, FOR PHILOSOPHY, IT WOULD BE HARD TO ARGUE AGAINST THE CLAIM TO THAT TITLE MADE ON BEHALF OF A CENTURY POPULATED BY THE LIKES OF GALILEO, BACON, DESCARTES, HOBBES, BOYLE, SPINOZA, LOCKE, LEIBNIZ, AND NEWTON – A CENTURY THAT SAW THE RISE OF MODERN METAPHYSICS AND EPISTEMOLOGY, REVOLUTIONARY PROGRESS IN THE UNDERSTANDING OF NATURE, AND NEW MODELS OF THE RELATIONSHIP BETWEEN CITIZENS AND THE STATE. WE MAY NO LONGER THINK IN PRECISELY THE SAME TERMS THAT GUIDED THESE EARLY MODERN THINKERS. BUT THE WAY IN WHICH WE LOOK AT THE WORLD AND AT OURSELVES HAS ITS ORIGINS IN THEIR HIGHLY CREATIVE ENDEAVORS, IN PHILO-SOPHICAL INQUIRY THAT FLOURISHED DESPITE – OR, MORE LIKELY, BE-CAUSE OF – THEIR INTELLECTUAL DIFFERENCES AND PERSONAL DISPUTES AND THE TURBULENT POLITICAL AND RELIGIOUS TIMES IN WHICH THEY LIVED.

WERE ALL OF THE PHILOSOPHERS IN THIS BOOK REALLY "HERETICS"? YES, IF THE TERM "HERESY" REFERS GENERALLY TO THE PROMOTION OF OPINIONS CONTRARY TO WHAT PASSES FOR CONVENTIONAL TRUTH, WHETHER IT BE IN SCIENCE, RELIGION, PHILOSOPHY, ECONOMICS, ETC.. SEVERAL WERE, IN FACT, OFFICIALLY DECLARED AS HERETICS BY ONE RELIGIOUS BODY OR ANOTHER. BRUNO AND GALILEO, OF COURSE, WERE PUNISHED ON JUST THESE GROUNDS BY THE CATHOLIC CHURCH; AND SPINOZA WAS EXCOMMUNICATED FOR HIS "ABOMINABLE HERESIES AND MONSTROUS DEEDS" FROM THE PORTUGUESE-JEWISH COMMUNITY OF AMSTERDAM. MOREOVER, PRACTICALLY EVERY ONE OF THE PHILOSOPHERS PORTRAYED HERE HAD WRITINGS BANNED BY THE VATICAN'S *INDEX OF PROHIBITED BOOKS*.

WORKS BY BRUNO, GALILEO, BACON, DESCARTES, HOBBES, PASCAL, SPINOZA, ARNAULD, MALEBRANCHE, BOYLE, LOCKE, LEIBNIZ, AND NEWTON ALL APPEAR ON THAT INFAMOUS LIST. RELIGIOUS AUTHORITIES IN THE MEDIEVAL AND EARLY MODERN PERIODS SOMETIMES HAD A HARD TIME DISTINGUISHING INDEPENDENT THINKING FROM HERESY.

IN THIS GRAPHIC BOOK, WE TELL THE STORY OF THE MOST BRILLIANT PERIOD IN PHILOSOPHY'S HISTORY. THE THINKERS WE PORTRAY DID NOT TOTALLY ABANDON THE CONCEPTUAL FRAMEWORKS OF THEIR FOREBEARS; EVEN INTELLECTUAL REVOLUTIONS AND "PARADIGM SHIFTS" MAINTAIN SOME ENGAGEMENT WITH THE PAST, AND THE DIVISIONS BETWEEN PERIODS OF HISTORY ARE ALWAYS MUCH CLEANER IN HINDSIGHT. A LOT OF THE PHILOSOPHY OF THE SEVENTEENTH CENTURY, AS RECENT SCHOLARSHIP HAS SHOWN, SOUGHT TO ASSIMILATE, MODIFY, OR UPDATE SCHOLASTIC THOUGHT RATHER THAN REJECT IT OUTRIGHT. AT THE SAME TIME, THESE EARLY MODERN THINKERS WERE, QUITE SELF-CONSCIOUSLY, OUT TO TRANSFORM PHILOSOPHY AND SET IT ON A NEW COURSE. FROM GALILEO AND DESCARTES IN THE FIRST DECADES OF THE SEVENTEENTH CENTURY TO LEIBNIZ AND NEWTON AT THE TURN OF THE EIGHTEENTH, THESE ARE SOME TRULY WONDROUS BEGINNINGS.

ROME

1600

THE 17TH CENTURY DID NOT START OUT WELL FOR PHILOSOPHY.

GIORDANO BRUNO HAD BEEN TEACHING THAT THE EARTH IS NOT THE CENTER OF THE UNIVERSE,

AND THAT THE STARS WERE SUNS WITH PLANETS ORBITING THEM.

HIS THEOLOGICAL AND POLITICAL VIEWS WERE ALSO HIGHLY UNORTHODOX.

HE WAS DECLARED A HERETIC BY THE ROMAN INQUISITION AND SENTENCED TO DEATH.

ON FEBRUARY 17, 1600, IN THE CAMPO DE' FIORI IN ROME, GIORDANO BRUNO WAS BURNED ALIVE AT THE STAKE.

ROME

1633

THREE DECADES LATER, THE CATHOLIC CHURCH STILL KEPT AN EYE ON WHAT PHILOSOPHERS WERE SAYING ABOUT THE COSMOS.

WHEN GALILEO GALILEI WAS A YOUNG PROFESSOR AT THE UNIVERSITY OF PISA...

HE WAS INTERESTED MAINLY IN PHYSICS AND THE MOTION OF BODIES.

HMM...

BODIES FALLING FROM THE SAME HEIGHT WILL DESCEND AT EXACTLY THE SAME RATE AND HIT THE GROUND AT THE SAME TIME...

WATCH OUT!

...REGARDLESS OF WEIGHT.

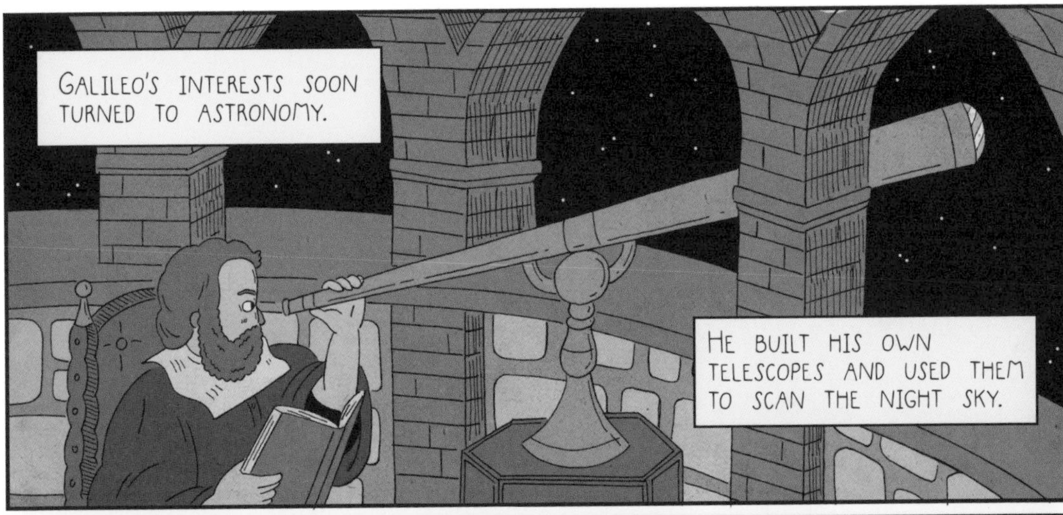
GALILEO'S INTERESTS SOON TURNED TO ASTRONOMY.
HE BUILT HIS OWN TELESCOPES AND USED THEM TO SCAN THE NIGHT SKY.

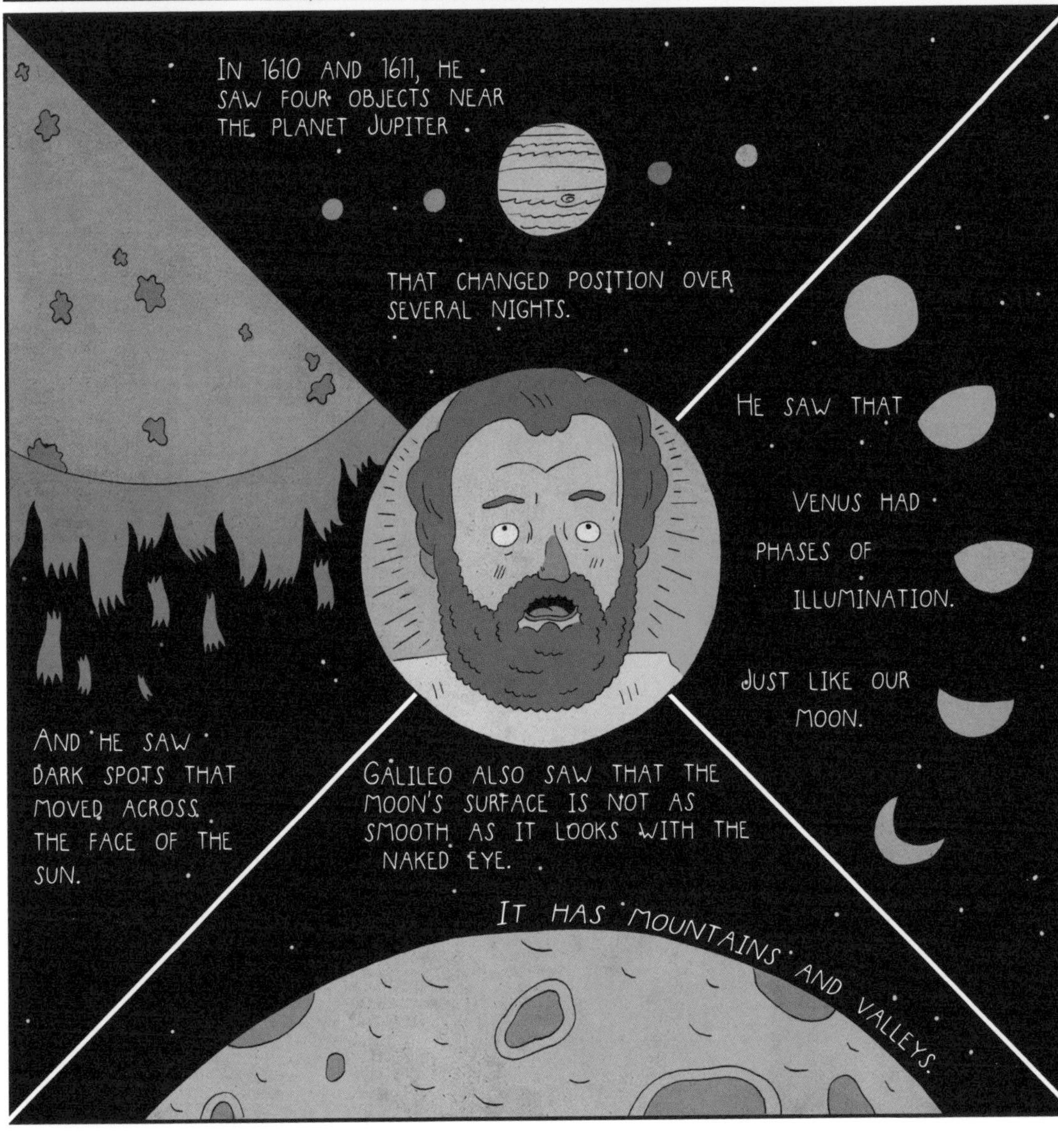
IN 1610 AND 1611, HE SAW FOUR OBJECTS NEAR THE PLANET JUPITER
THAT CHANGED POSITION OVER SEVERAL NIGHTS.
HE SAW THAT
VENUS HAD PHASES OF ILLUMINATION.
JUST LIKE OUR MOON.
AND HE SAW DARK SPOTS THAT MOVED ACROSS THE FACE OF THE SUN.
GALILEO ALSO SAW THAT THE MOON'S SURFACE IS NOT AS SMOOTH AS IT LOOKS WITH THE NAKED EYE.
IT HAS MOUNTAINS AND VALLEYS.

GALILEO FOUND ALL THIS TO BE EVIDENCE THAT THE HEAVENS ARE NOT AS UNIFORM AND PERFECT AS EVERYONE THOUGHT.

COPERNICUS WAS RIGHT: THE EARTH IS NOT SO SPECIAL.

IT IS NOT THE CENTER OF THE COSMOS; IT IS A PLANET JUST LIKE THE OTHERS, AND THEY ALL ORBIT THE SUN.

IN 1616, POPE PAUL V CONDEMNED COPERNICUS'S THEORY AS HERESY. ACCORDING TO THE BIBLE, HE SAID, THE SUN AND ALL THE PLANETS GO AROUND THE EARTH.

THE COPERNICAN THEORY MUST BE ABANDONED!

BUT GALILEO, NOW THE MATHEMATICIAN AND PHILOSOPHER TO THE GRAND DUKE OF TUSCANY, COULD NOT HELP HIMSELF.

(GRUMBLE, GRUMBLE) I'LL SHOW *THEM* COPERNICAN THEORY.

IN 1632, HE PUBLISHED

DIALOGUE CONCERNING TWO CHIEF WORLD SYSTEMS

GALILEO

A VIGOROUS DEFENSE OF COPERNICANISM.

THE HELIOCENTRIC THEORY DOES A MUCH BETTER JOB OF EXPLAINING THE PHENOMENA IN THE HEAVENS AND ON EARTH.

THE CHURCH WAS NOT AMUSED.

THE NEW POPE, URBAN VIII, WHILE SYMPATHETIC TO GALILEO, WAS ANGRY THAT THE ASTRONOMER HAD DISOBEYED THE CHURCH'S EARLIER ORDER.

GALILEO!

HERETIC!

YOU LEAVE ME NO CHOICE!

GALILEO WAS PUNISHED WITH HOUSE ARREST FOR THE REST OF HIS LIFE, AND HIS BOOK WAS BANNED.

STILL, HE KNEW HE WAS RIGHT.

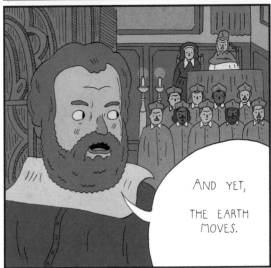

AND YET, THE EARTH MOVES.

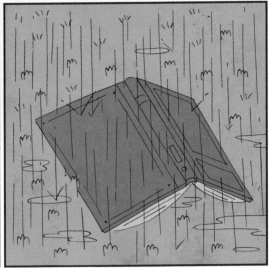

MEANWHILE, IN HOLLAND, A FRENCH PHILOSOPHER WAS ABOUT TO PUBLISH HIS FIRST BOOK.

RENÉ DESCARTES HAD MOVED TO THE LAND OF MILK AND WINDMILLS TO DO HIS WORK WITHOUT DISTRACTIONS.

AMSTERDAM IS A NICE CITY. BUT I CAN'T GET ANY WORK DONE WITH ALL THIS NOISE.

AH, MUCH BETTER OUT HERE IN THE PEACE AND QUIET OF THE DUTCH COUNTRYSIDE.

HIS BOOK *THE WORLD* WOULD SHOW HOW HIS NEW PHILOSOPHY CAN EXPLAIN "ALL THE PHENOMENA OF NATURE."

MOST THINKERS OF THE TIME TOOK THEIR LEAD FROM THE ANCIENT GREEK PHILOSO-PHER ARISTOTLE. THEY BELIEVED THAT NATURAL BODIES ARE COMPOSED OF MATTER AND FORM.

SO DREAMY!

A TRUE GENIUS!

MATTER IS THE PHYSICAL STUFF OF ANY BODY. FORMS ARE MORE LIKE SOULS; THEY ARE ACTIVE SPIRITUAL POWERS THAT EXPLAIN WHY THINGS LOOK AND BEHAVE AS THEY DO.

AN APPLE FALLS TO THE GROUND BECAUSE IT HAS THE FORM "HEAVINESS" THAT MAKES IT SEEK THE CENTER OF THE EARTH. A HORSE LOOKS AND ACTS LIKE IT DOES BECAUSE IT HAS THE FORM "HORSENESS."

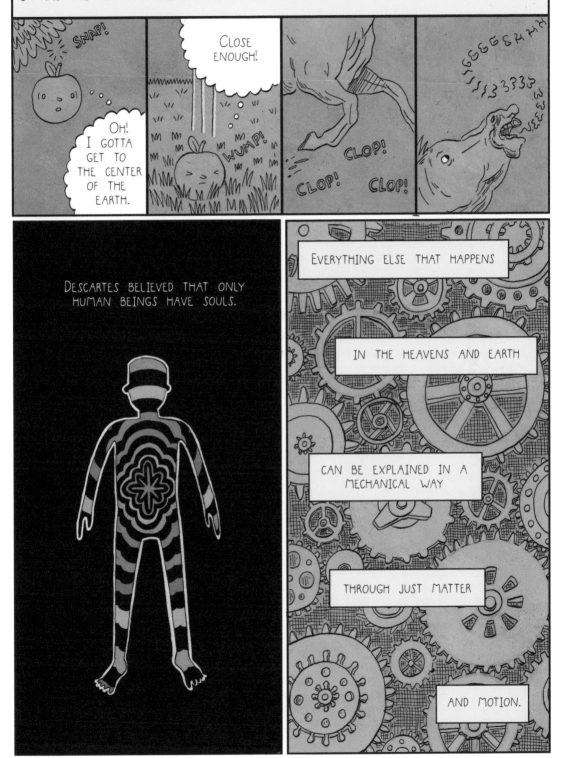

SNAP!

OH! I GOTTA GET TO THE CENTER OF THE EARTH.

CLOSE ENOUGH!

WUMP!

CLOP! CLOP! CLOP! CLOP!

DESCARTES BELIEVED THAT ONLY HUMAN BEINGS HAVE SOULS.

EVERYTHING ELSE THAT HAPPENS

IN THE HEAVENS AND EARTH

CAN BE EXPLAINED IN A MECHANICAL WAY

THROUGH JUST MATTER

AND MOTION.

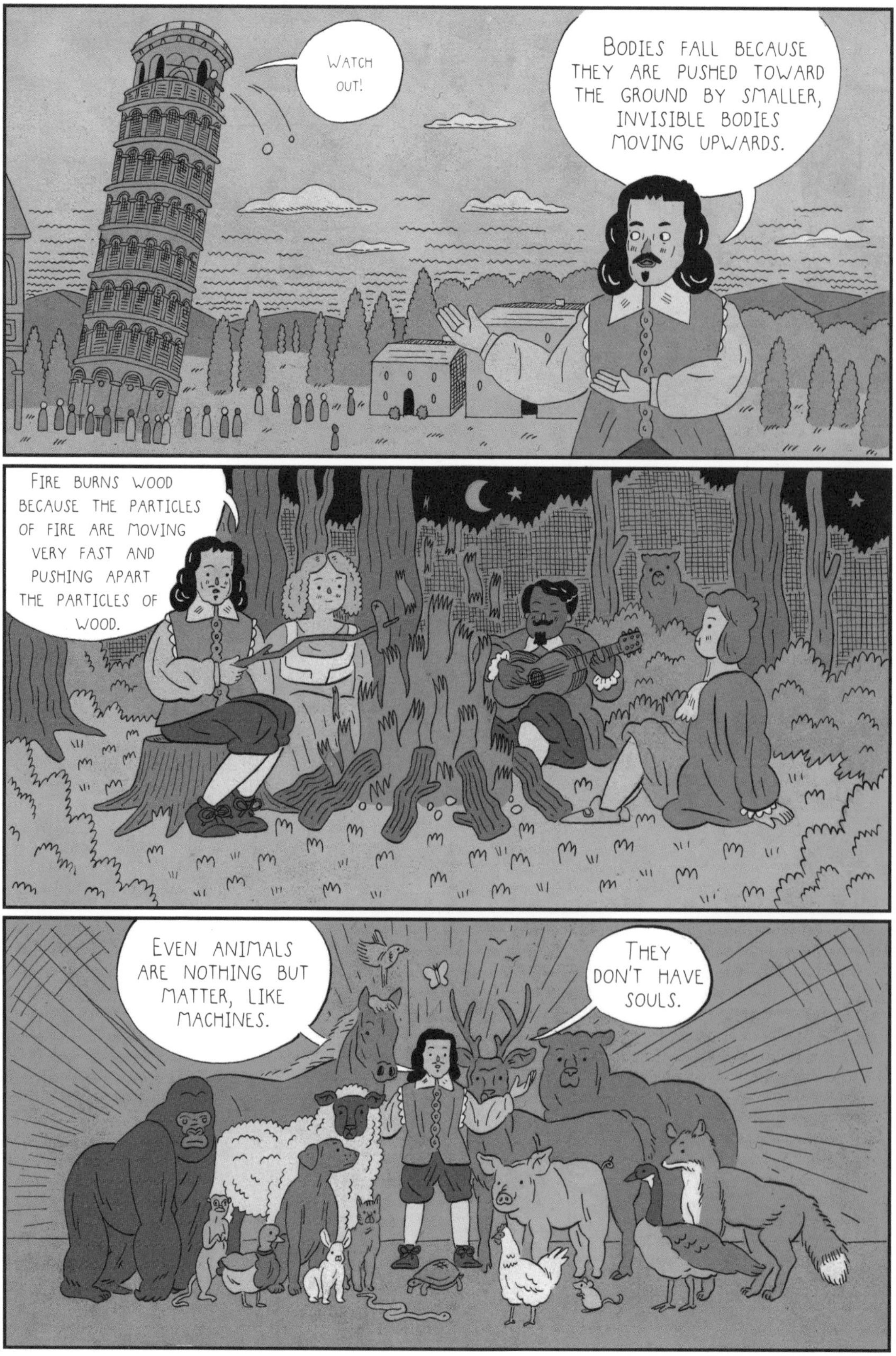
WATCH OUT!
BODIES FALL BECAUSE THEY ARE PUSHED TOWARD THE GROUND BY SMALLER, INVISIBLE BODIES MOVING UPWARDS.
FIRE BURNS WOOD BECAUSE THE PARTICLES OF FIRE ARE MOVING VERY FAST AND PUSHING APART THE PARTICLES OF WOOD.
EVEN ANIMALS ARE NOTHING BUT MATTER, LIKE MACHINES.
THEY DON'T HAVE SOULS.

IN HIS BOOK, DESCARTES ALSO PRESENTED A HELIOCENTRIC VIEW OF THE COSMOS, WITH THE EARTH AND ALL THE OTHER PLANETS MOVED AROUND THE SUN OF MATTER. BY SPINNING VORTICES

IF THE COPERNICAN VIEW IS FALSE, THEN SO IS MY ENTIRE PHILOSOPHY.

ONE DAY IN 1633, DESCARTES WAS LOOKING FOR A COPY OF GALILEO'S *DIALOGUE* IN AN AMSTERDAM BOOKSTORE.

SORRY, BUT I DON'T HAVE ANY COPIES. THE BOOK WAS BURNED IN ROME.

DESCARTES DECIDED NOT TO PUBLISH *THE WORLD* AFTER ALL.

ZUT ALORS!

I DON'T WANT TO GET INTO TROUBLE TOO!

LEIDEN

1640

LIKE GALILEO, DESCARTES WAS NOT ONE TO GIVE UP EASILY.

HE CONTINUED HIS SCIENTIFIC AND MATHEMATICAL WORK, PUBLISHING ESSAYS ON GEOMETRY...

GEOMETRIC FIGURES CAN BE REPRESENTED AS ALGEBRAIC EQUATIONS!

LIGHT IS AN IMPULSE FROM A LUMINOUS BODY COMMUNICATED THROUGH THE MATTER OF THE AIR.

ON OPTICS...

AND EVEN ON METEOROLOGY...

A RAINBOW IS NOT A SIGN FROM GOD. IT IS JUST THE REFRACTION OF LIGHT AS IT PASSES THROUGH WATER DROPLETS IN THE SKY!

ALONG WITH THE *DISCOURSE ON METHOD*.

IF YOU WANT TO UNDERSTAND THE TRUE NATURE OF THINGS, FORGET WHAT PHILOSOPHICAL TRADITION SAYS AND THINK FOR YOURSELF.

USE YOUR SENSES! USE YOUR INTELLECT!

DESCARTES'S GOAL WAS A BODY OF SCIENTIFIC KNOWLEDGE THAT HAD THE SAME DEGREE OF CERTAINTY AS THE TRUTHS OF MATHEMATICS.

ADIEU, ARISTOTLE!

DESCARTES KNEW HE WAS NOT THE FIRST TO INSIST THAT SCIENCE SHOULD PROCEED BY SELF-DIRECTED INQUIRY RATHER THAN BLIND FEALTY TO ANCIENT AUTHORITY.

FRANCIS BACON WAS AN ENGLISH NATURAL PHILOSOPHER, LAWYER, AND STATESMAN.

I NOW APPOINT YOU LORD CHANCELLOR OF THE REALM OF ENGLAND.

IN HIS *NEW ORGANON*, BACON DISTINGUISHES TRUE SCIENTIFIC METHOD FROM THE UNWARRANTED SPECULATIONS AND STERILE ARGUMENTS OF EARLIER PHILOSOPHIES.

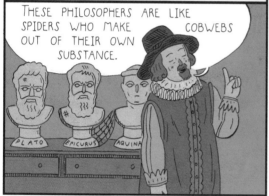

THESE PHILOSOPHERS ARE LIKE SPIDERS WHO MAKE COBWEBS OUT OF THEIR OWN SUBSTANCE.

HE BELIEVED THAT THE INTERPRETATION OF NATURE SHOULD BE GROUNDED IN SENSE EXPERIENCE, NOT DEDUCED FROM METAPHYSICAL CONJECTURES.

WE MUST LOOK TO THE FACTS THEMSELVES!

HOWEVER, THERE ARE THE "IDOLS" OF HUMAN UNDERSTANDING - PREJUDICES THAT INHIBIT TRUE INQUIRY - FROM WHICH WE MUST FIRST LIBERATE OURSELVES.

THEY SO BESET THE MIND THAT TRUTH CAN HARDLY ENTER THERE.

IDOLS OF THE TRIBE ORIGINATE IN HUMAN NATURE, AND SO ARE COMMON TO ALL HUMAN BEINGS.

LOOK HOW THE CELESTIAL BODIES MOVE IN PERFECT CIRCLES!

IDOLS OF THE CAVE ARE IRRATIONAL BIASES THAT A PERSON ACQUIRES OVER A LIFETIME.

IDOLS OF THE MARKET ARISE THROUGH CONFUSIONS IN THE USE OF LANGUAGE.

AND IDOLS OF THE THEATER ARE ESTABLISHED WHEN PEOPLE UNCRITICALLY RECEIVE PHILOSOPHICAL THEORIES AS ABSOLUTE TRUTHS.

ACCORDING TO BACON, THE PROPER METHOD FOR STUDYING NATURE AND LEARNING ITS SECRETS IS INDUCTIVE REASONING.

IT BEGINS WITH A METHODICAL AND GUIDED GATHERING OF RAW DATA THROUGH OBSERVATION.

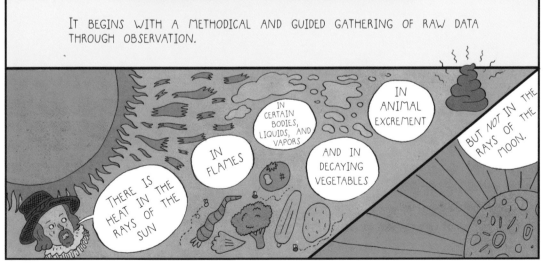

EXPERIMENTATION PROVIDES EVEN MORE DATA...

WILL THE RAYS OF THE MOON BECOME WARM IF THEY PASS THROUGH A MAGNIFYING GLASS?

...AND REVEALS NEW CONNECTIONS.

MOTION INCREASES HEAT, AS WE SEE FROM THE BLOWING OF A BELLOWS.

WITH A CAREFULLY COMPILED AND THOROUGH "HISTORY," THE NATURAL PHILOSOPHER CAN FORMULATE GENERAL "AXIOMS" OR HYPOTHESES.

HEAT IS NOT THE SAME AS LIGHT, SINCE FIRE AND BOILING WATER ARE BOTH INSTANCES OF HEAT BUT NOT OF LIGHT.

BUT THERE IS MOTION IN BOTH FIRE

AND BOILING WATER.

IS HEAT JUST MOTION?

THESE ARE THEN TESTED BY FURTHER OBSERVATION AND EXPERIMENT.

SLOWLY AND BY DEGREES, HE WILL COME TO KNOW THE TRUE NATURE OF THE PHENOMENON.

IT APPEARS THAT HEAT IS A PARTICULAR KIND OF MOTION.

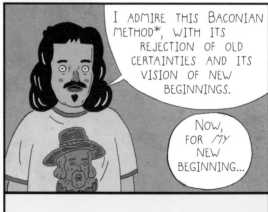

I ADMIRE THIS BACONIAN METHOD*, WITH ITS REJECTION OF OLD CERTAINTIES AND ITS VISION OF NEW BEGINNINGS.

NOW, FOR *MY* NEW BEGINNING...

*YES, HE REALLY DID USE THIS PHRASE.

WITH THE MECHANICAL PHILOSOPHY, DESCARTES WOULD EXPLAIN EVERYTHING IN THE TERRESTRIAL AND CELESTIAL REALMS IN TERMS FAMILIAR FROM EVERYDAY EXPERIENCE.

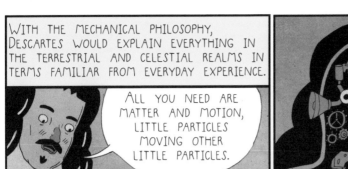

ALL YOU NEED ARE MATTER AND MOTION, LITTLE PARTICLES MOVING OTHER LITTLE PARTICLES.

EVEN OUR OWN BODIES ARE JUST LIKE MACHINES.

HEY, THAT DEVICE HASN'T BEEN INVENTED YET!

LIGHTEN UP, NEWTON.

DESCARTES RECOGNIZED, HOWEVER, THAT HE WAS SKIPPING AN IMPORTANT PHILOSOPHICAL STEP.

IS SCIENCE EVEN POSSIBLE?

HOW CAN I KNOW THAT I CAN KNOW IF I DON'T KNOW WHAT IT IS TO KNOW?

I THINK YOU'VE HAD ENOUGH TO DRINK.

23

SCIENCE MUST BE GROUNDED IN "FIRST PRINCIPLES." AND AMONG THESE MOST FUNDAMENTAL STARTING POINTS IS KNOWLEDGE ABOUT KNOWLEDGE ITSELF.

THIS IS THE PROJECT OF EPISTEMOLOGY.

A PHILOSOPHER SHOULD, AT LEAST ONCE IN LIFE, EXAMINE WHAT TRUE KNOWLEDGE *(SCIENTIA)* IS AND HOW IT CAN BE ACHIEVED.

PHILOSOPHY IS LIKE A TREE:

AND THE BRANCHES ARE ALL THE OTHER SCIENCES, MEDICINE, AND ETHICS.

THE ROOTS ARE METAPHYSICS.

THE TRUNK IS PHYSICS.

WHAT DO I KNOW?

HOW DO I KNOW?

WHAT *CAN* I KNOW?

ALSO AMONG FIRST PRINCIPLES ARE CERTAIN TRUTHS OF METAPHYSICS THAT ARE PRIOR TO KNOWING ANYTHING ELSE.

WHAT IS A BODY?

WHAT IS A SOUL?

WHAT AM I?

DESCARTES TAKES UP THESE EPISTEMOLOGICAL AND METAPHYSICAL QUESTIONS IN HIS MOST FAMOUS WORK.

WITH THE *MEDITATIONS*, DESCARTES BEGINS HIS GRAND SCIENTIFIC PROJECT FROM PHILOSOPHICAL SCRATCH. HE DOES NOT TAKE ANYTHING FOR GRANTED.

DO I KNOW *ANYTHING* WITH ABSOLUTE CERTAINTY?

HE STARTS WITH WHAT SEEMS TO BE THE MOST OBVIOUS SOURCE OF KNOWLEDGE.

MY SENSES TELL ME THAT ROSES ARE RED,

VIOLETS BLUE,

FIRE HOT,

AND TENNIS BALLS ROUND.

BUT IS THE WORLD ALWAYS AND TRULY AS IT APPEARS TO BE?

OF COURSE NOT —

OBVIOUSLY MY SENSES SOMETIMES MISLEAD ME.

YOU CANNOT *ALWAYS* BELIEVE WHAT YOU SEE!

STILL, EVEN IF MY SENSES OCCASIONALLY DECEIVE ME ABOUT OBJECTS THAT ARE SMALL OR FAR AWAY,

THEY TELL ME MANY OTHER THINGS THAT I CANNOT POSSIBLY DOUBT.

THEY TELL ME THAT I AM SITTING HERE

BY THE FIRE,

WEARING A WINTER DRESSING-GOWN,

WITH THIS PIECE OF PAPER IN MY HANDS.

AND YET...

HAVE I FORGOTTEN HOW MUCH MY DREAMS SEEM LIKE WAKING EXPERIENCES?

SO HOW DO I KNOW THAT I AM NOT RIGHT NOW ONLY DREAMING THAT I HAVE A BODY?

MAYBE I AM *ALWAYS* DREAMING AND THERE ARE NO BODIES AT ALL!

PERHAPS *ALL* OF MY SENSE EXPERIENCE IS BUT A DREAM-LIKE ILLUSION!

NONETHELESS, DREAMING OR NOT, THERE SEEM TO BE AT LEAST SOME THINGS THAT CAN BE KNOWN FOR CERTAIN.

EVEN IF THERE IS NO EXTERNAL WORLD AT ALL - NO BODIES, NOT EVEN MY OWN - CAN'T I AT LEAST ACCEPT ALL THOSE ABSTRACT TRUTHS THAT I PERCEIVE WITH MY INTELLECT?

WHETHER I AM WIDE AWAKE OR MERELY DREAMING,

ONE PLUS ONE EQUALS TWO.

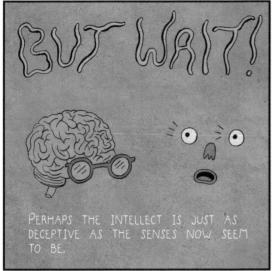

BUT WAIT!

Perhaps the intellect is just as deceptive as the senses now seem to be.

What if I was created by an evil, deceiving God or a demon hell-bent on seeing me go wrong whenever I use my reason?

How can I trust an intellect that was given to me by a malevolent creator?

Maybe everything I thought was true about the world and about science and mathematics is just an illusion.

This play is terrible.

Maybe one plus one does not really equal two!

Maybe *nothing at all* can be known!

OMD!*

Have I gone too far?

*Oh *mon dieu*!

Descartes's certainty in his own existence is immune to doubt, at least as long as he is thinking.

It does not matter what he is thinking of.

Descartes may not yet know if he has a body – the existence of an external, material world is still in doubt.

But what he cannot doubt is that he, a thinking thing, exists.

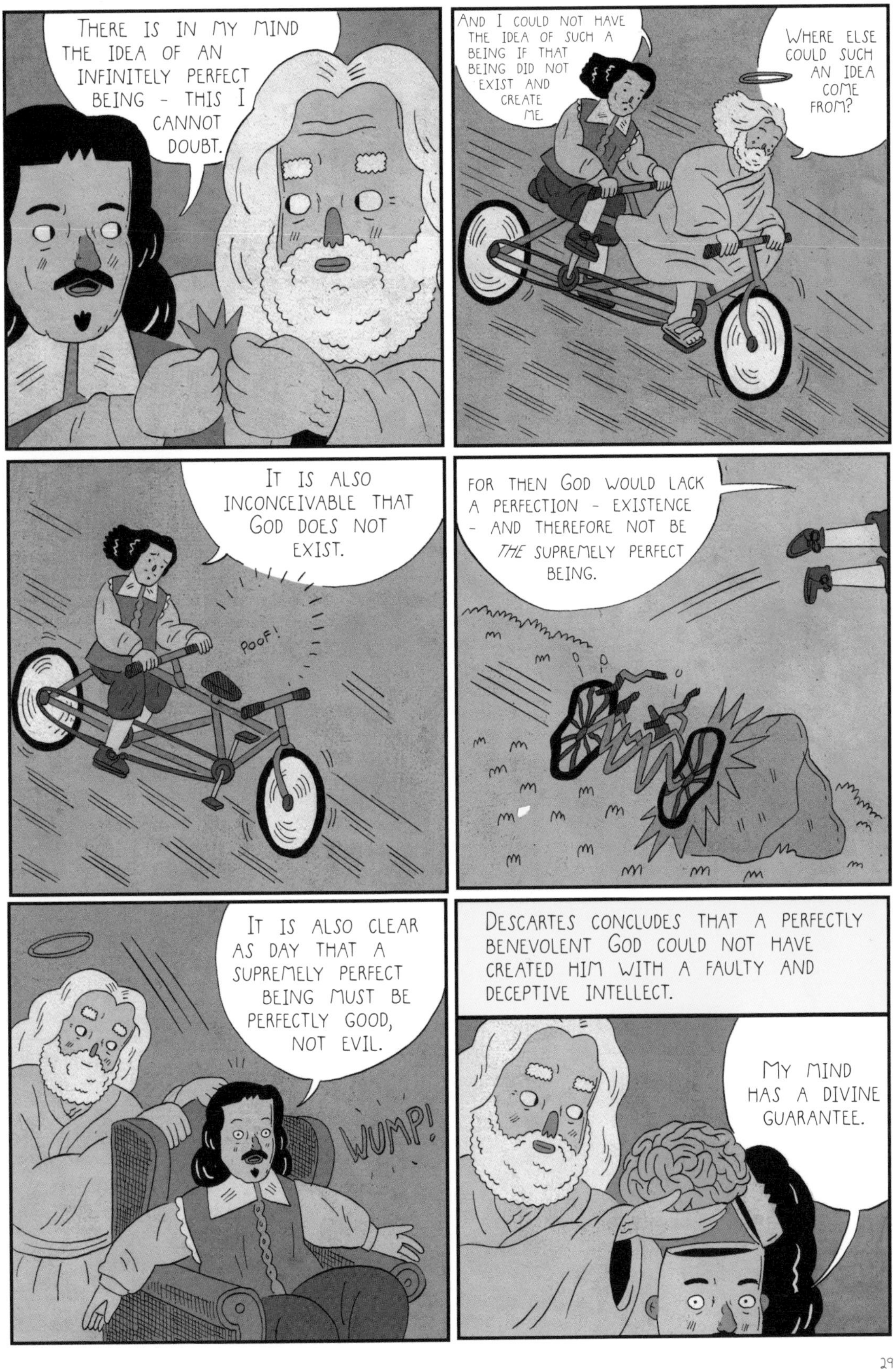
THERE IS IN MY MIND THE IDEA OF AN INFINITELY PERFECT BEING - THIS I CANNOT DOUBT.
AND I COULD NOT HAVE THE IDEA OF SUCH A BEING IF THAT BEING DID NOT EXIST AND CREATE ME.
WHERE ELSE COULD SUCH AN IDEA COME FROM?
IT IS ALSO INCONCEIVABLE THAT GOD DOES NOT EXIST.
POOF!
FOR THEN GOD WOULD LACK A PERFECTION - EXISTENCE - AND THEREFORE NOT BE *THE* SUPREMELY PERFECT BEING.
IT IS ALSO CLEAR AS DAY THAT A SUPREMELY PERFECT BEING MUST BE PERFECTLY GOOD, NOT EVIL.
WUMP!
DESCARTES CONCLUDES THAT A PERFECTLY BENEVOLENT GOD COULD NOT HAVE CREATED HIM WITH A FAULTY AND DECEPTIVE INTELLECT.
MY MIND HAS A DIVINE GUARANTEE.

I NOW KNOW THAT WHEN I USE MY GOD-GIVEN INTELLECT PROPERLY AND CAREFULLY,

AND ASSENT ONLY TO WHAT I CLEARLY AND DISTINCTLY PERCEIVE TO BE TRUE BY THE NATURAL LIGHT OF REASON,

I WILL HAVE TRUE KNOWLEDGE.

DESCARTES THEN SEES THAT THERE ARE A NUMBER OF THINGS THAT HE DOES CLEARLY AND DISTINCTLY PERCEIVE.

I KNOW THAT BODIES REALLY DO EXIST.

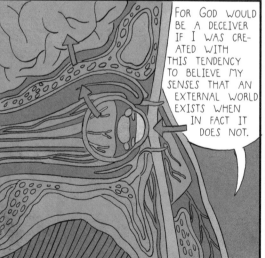

FOR GOD WOULD BE A DECEIVER IF I WAS CREATED WITH THIS TENDENCY TO BELIEVE MY SENSES THAT AN EXTERNAL WORLD EXISTS WHEN IN FACT IT DOES NOT.

BUT THE WORLD OF BODIES IS NOT EXACTLY WHAT IT APPEARS TO THE SENSES TO BE.

ROSES ARE NOT REALLY RED, VIOLETS ARE NOT REALLY BLUE, AND FIRE IS NOT REALLY HOT.

THE INTELLECT'S CONCEPT OF "BODY" INCLUDES ONLY THE PROPERTIES OF EXTENSION. TO BE A BODY IS JUST TO BE A GEOMETRICAL OBJECT.

I ALSO CLEARLY AND DISTINCTLY PERCEIVE THAT I AM A THINKING THING DISTINCT FROM MY BODY, AND COULD EVEN EXIST WITHOUT IT.

ACCORDING TO DESCARTES, THERE ARE ONLY TWO KINDS OF THINGS IN THE WORLD — MENTAL THINGS AND PHYSICAL THINGS — AND THEY HAVE NOTHING WHATSOEVER IN COMMON.

SOUL OR MIND IS THINKING SUBSTANCE, AND ITS MODES OR PROPERTIES ARE IDEAS AND VOLITIONS.

BODY IS EXTENDED SUBSTANCE. ITS MODES ARE SHAPE, SIZE, DIVISIBILITY, AND MOTION OR REST.

MINDS HAVE NONE OF THE PROPERTIES THAT BELONG TO BODIES, AND BODIES HAVE NONE OF THE PROPERTIES THAT BELONG TO MINDS.

THE RED I SEE WHEN I LOOK AT A ROSE, LIKE THE HEAT I FEEL WHEN MY HAND IS NEAR A FIRE, IS ONLY A SENSORY PERCEPTION IN MY MIND.

WITH THIS MIND-BODY *DUALISM* COMES A MECHANISTIC PHYSICS — A SCIENCE OF NATURE THAT INVOLVES ONLY THE TRUE MATHEMATICAL FEATURES OF BODIES.

ALL YOU NEED IS GEOMETRY AND LAWS OF MOTION.

SOME BODIES ARE SPECIAL, HOWEVER.

I AM A THINKING THING, AND BODIES DO NOT THINK. BUT I KNOW FROM EVERYDAY EXPERIENCE THAT THIS BODY IS UNITED WITH A THINKING SOUL.

ALRIGHT, YOU'RE GOOD TO GO.

IT IS A VERY CLOSE RELATIONSHIP.

MY SOUL IS NOT IN THE BODY LIKE A SAILOR IN A SHIP. MY SOUL AND MY BODY ARE INTERMINGLED IN A REAL UNION.

WHEN I PRICK MYSELF, I IMMEDIATELY FEEL PAIN.

WHEN I WILL TO RAISE MY ARM,

IT STRAIGHTAWAY RISES.

SUCH WONDERFUL EVIDENCE OF GOD'S PROVIDENTIAL WISDOM!

NOT EVERYONE WAS SO ENAMORED OF DESCARTES'S NEW PHILOSOPHY.

GOD'S PROVIDENTIAL WISDOM?

THE MATHEMATICIAN AND RELIGIOUS THINKER BLAISE PASCAL, FOR ONE, DID NOT SHARE DESCARTES'S CONFIDENCE IN THE POWER OF HUMAN REASON.

CAN OUR INTELLECT REALLY LEAD US TO KNOWLEDGE OF GOD AND THE SOUL?

PASCAL HAD A RATHER DARK AND PESSIMISTIC VIEW OF HUMAN NATURE.

WE ARE MERE THINKING REEDS.

OUR GREATNESS LIES ONLY IN OUR ABILITY TO RECOGNIZE OUR OWN INSIGNIFICANCE AND WRETCHEDNESS BEFORE AN INFINITE GOD.

SALVATION COMES THROUGH FAITH. REASON CANNOT BRING YOU CLOSER TO GOD. IT CANNOT EVEN PROVE GOD'S EXISTENCE.

STILL, I DO KNOW THAT I'M BETTER OFF BELIEVING THAT GOD EXISTS.

PASCAL SEES IT AS A KIND OF WAGER.

LET'S SAY I DO NOT BELIEVE IN GOD.

THEN IF GOD DOES NOT EXIST - GREAT, I HAVE A TRUE BELIEF, BUT THAT'S NOT MUCH OF A PAYOFF.

BUT IF I DO NOT BELIEVE IN GOD AND GOD *DOES* EXIST,

THEN I AM IN DEEP TROUBLE.

MY LOSS WILL BE INFINITE - ETERNAL DAMNATION.

ON THE OTHER HAND, IF I *DO* BELIEVE IN GOD AND IF GOD *DOES* EXIST, THEN MY REWARD IS INFINITE - ETERNAL SALVATION.

HIT ME.

I KNOW WHERE I'M PUTTING MY MONEY.

ONE DAY WHEN PASCAL WAS SICK IN BED, DESCARTES, ON A VISIT TO PARIS, CAME TO SEE HIM.

BLAISE!

RENÉ!

THEY TALKED ABOUT WHETHER A VACUUM IS POSSIBLE IN NATURE.

OUI!

MAIS NON! IF A BODY IS JUST EXTENSION, THEN ANY 3D SPACE IS A BODY.

AND PASCAL SHOWED DESCARTES THE ADDING MACHINE HE HAD INVENTED.

TRÈS COOL!

REGARDEZ!

BUT THEIR CONVERSATION MUST ALSO HAVE TURNED TOWARD MATTERS OF FAITH AND REASON.

DON'T YOU SEE THAT THE HEART HAS ITS REASONS THAT REASON CANNOT SEE?

PASCAL'S AUSTERE CHRISTIAN FAITH KEPT HIM FROM APPRECIATING DESCARTES'S RATIONALISM.

YOU NEED SOUP AND REST.

FOR OTHERS, THE PROBLEM WAS DESCARTES'S METAPHYSICS, ESPECIALLY HIS ACCOUNT OF MIND AND BODY.

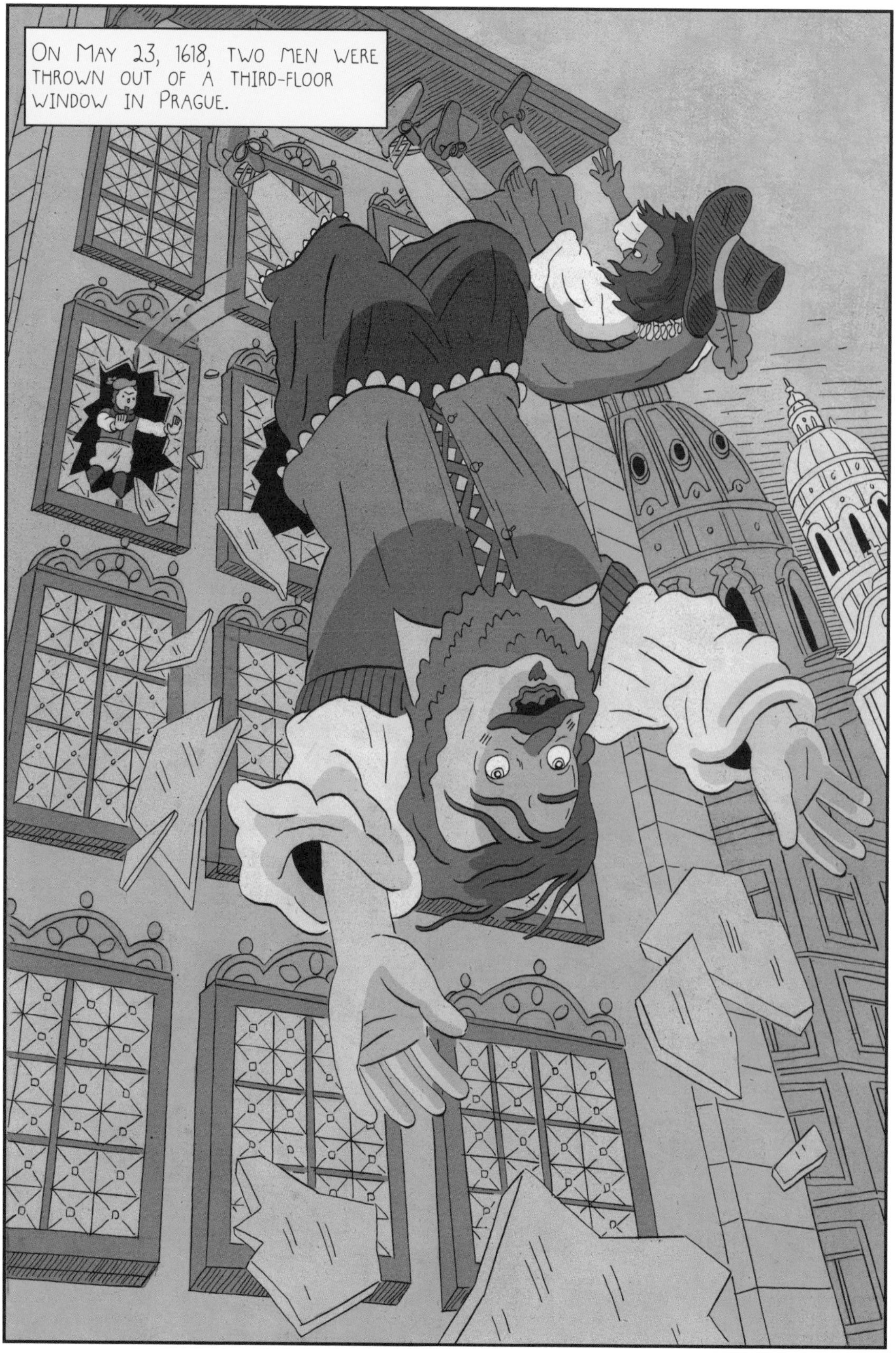
ON MAY 23, 1618, TWO MEN WERE THROWN OUT OF A THIRD-FLOOR WINDOW IN PRAGUE.

THIS RUDE RECEPTION OF THE AMBASSADORS OF FERDINAND II, THE CATHOLIC KING OF BOHEMIA, BY DISGRUNTLED PROTESTANT SUBJECTS

WOULD LEAD TO THIRTY YEARS OF WAR ACROSS EUROPE.

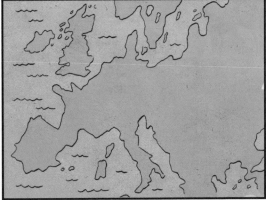

THE BOHEMIANS ASKED A PROTESTANT, FREDERICK V OF PALATINE, TO BE THEIR NEW KING.

BUT FREDERICK WAS QUICKLY DEPOSED BY FERDINAND'S ARMY

AND FLED WITH HIS FAMILY TO HOLLAND.

SEVERAL DECADES LATER, FREDERICK'S BRILLIANT DAUGHTER ELISABETH, A PRINCESS IN EXILE FAR FROM HER HOMELAND, WAS DEVOTING MUCH OF HER TIME TO PHILOSOPHY.

She was intrigued by Descartes's *Meditations*, but found some of his views puzzling.

Monsieur Descartes, I would be grateful if you could enlighten me.

How can the soul, being only a thinking substance,

move the body and bring about voluntary motions?

Bodies move only when pushed by other bodies,

and extension and physical contact are required for this.

But an immaterial soul does not have extension.

How, then, can it push a body?

DESCARTES, ANTICIPATING ROYAL PATRONAGE, WAS HAPPY TO ANSWER ELISABETH'S QUERY.

I AM HONORED THAT YOUR HIGHNESS HAS DEIGNED TO READ MY *MEDITATIONS*.

AND THE QUESTION YOU RAISE IS INDEED A DIFFICULT ONE.

WE KNOW FROM EVERYDAY EXPERIENCE THAT THE SOUL CAN ACT ON AND BE ACTED ON BY THE BODY.

BUT YOU SHOULD NOT TRY TO UNDERSTAND THIS CAUSAL INTERACTION IN TERMS OF PHYSICAL CONTACT, WHICH IS HOW WE UNDERSTAND THE INTERACTION OF BODIES.

THE MIND-BODY UNION IS A SPECIAL KIND OF RELATIONSHIP.

DESCARTES'S RESPONSE DID NOT RESOLVE ELISABETH'S PERPLEXITY.

"THE MIND-BODY UNION IS A SPECIAL KIND OF RELATIONSHIP"?

Perhaps, she suggested, mind and body are not so different after all.

THE NOTION THAT THE SOUL IS MATERIAL, A PART OF THE BODY, WAS ALSO RAISED BY ONE OF DESCARTES'S HARSHER CRITICS, THE ENGLISH PHILOSOPHER THOMAS HOBBES.

HOBBES AND DESCARTES SIMPLY DID NOT LIKE EACH OTHER.

DING! DING!

AND BENEATH THE PERSONAL ANIMOSITY WAS A FUNDAMENTAL METAPHYSICAL DISAGREEMENT.

HOLD ON, NOW! WE BOTH SUBSCRIBE TO THE MECHANICAL PHILOSOPHY.

YES, BUT HOBBES BELIEVED THAT THERE IS NOTHING IN THE WORLD BUT BODIES. THERE ARE NO INCORPOREAL SUBSTANCES.

I CERTAINLY GRANT THAT YOU ARE A THINKING THING.

BUT I BELIEVE THAT THIS THING THAT THINKS IS MADE OF MATTER.

DID YOU NOT FOLLOW MY ARGUMENT?

OF COURSE I DID.

SOMEBODY HIT SOMEONE!

IF I AM THINKING,

THEN THERE MUST BE A SUBJECT DOING THE THINKING,

AND THEREFORE I EXIST.

BUT THE SUBJECT OF AN ACTION HAS TO BE A CORPOREAL THING.

IN HIS OWN TREATISE ON HUMAN NATURE, POLITICS, AND RELIGION, TITLED *LEVIATHAN*, HOBBES CLAIMED THAT THE MIND AND ITS ACTIVITY IS JUST MATTER IN MOTION.

THERE IS NO SUCH THING AS A SOUL DISTINCT FROM THE BODY.

HOBBES'S MATERIALISM EXTENDED TO ALL STATES OF CONSCIOUSNESS.

OUR IDEAS, OUR SENSE PERCEPTIONS, OUR FEELINGS, OUR IMAGININGS, OUR VOLITIONS - THEY ARE ALL JUST MOTIONS IN THE BODY.

DESCARTES HAD LITTLE PATIENCE FOR PEOPLE LIKE HOBBES.

THIS ENGLISHMAN IS A NASTY PIECE OF WORK. I'D BEST NOT HAVE ANYTHING MORE TO DO WITH HIM, OR WE WILL BECOME ENEMIES.

PARIS

1646

IN THE 1640S, THOMAS HOBBES HAD MORE PRESSING MATTERS TO DEAL WITH THAN MIND-BODY METAPHYSICS.

GOOD RIDDANCE.

HE WAS IN PARIS TO DEBATE THE MERITS OF DESCARTES'S PHILOSOPHY BECAUSE THERE WAS CIVIL WAR ON THE HORIZON IN ENGLAND.

WITH PARLIAMENT PITTED AGAINST KING CHARLES I, HOBBES - A ROYALIST AND FEARING FOR HIS SAFETY AS THE KING'S ENEMIES GAINED THE UPPER HAND -

THE KING SHOULD NOT HAVE TO ANSWER TO ANYONE!

HAD GONE INTO EXILE IN 1640.

I GOTTA GET OUT OF HERE.

HE WROTE *LEVIATHAN* TO SHOW THAT THE AUTHORITY OF A SOVEREIGN MUST BE ABSOLUTE.

HE BEGAN HIS ARGUMENT BY DEPICTING A LIFE WITHOUT ANY GOVERNMENT.

IT'S NOT A PRETTY PICTURE.

IMAGINE A TIME WHEN THERE IS NO COMMONWEALTH, NO ORGANIZED SOCIETY, NO JUSTICE –

JUST A LOT OF PEOPLE LIVING WITHOUT LAWS OR LEADERS.

NOTHING TO KEEP THEM FROM CHEATING, STEALING,

OR EVEN KILLING EACH OTHER.

IN SUCH A CONDITION, EVERY MAN HAS A RIGHT TO EVERYTHING, EVEN ANOTHER'S BODY.

IF I CAN GET IT, IT'S MINE.

IF YOU CAN TAKE IT FROM ME, IT'S YOURS.

EVERYONE IS ACTING ONLY FOR THEIR OWN WELFARE. MOTIVATED BY FEAR, EACH DOES WHAT THEY CAN TO SURVIVE.

IN THE STATE OF NATURE, MIGHT MAKES RIGHT, AND LIFE WILL BE SOLITARY, POOR, NASTY, BRUTISH, AND SHORT.

THESE PEOPLE ARE FRIGHTENED BUT RATIONAL.

THEY REALIZE THAT IF THEY ARE GOING TO SURVIVE AND FLOURISH, THEY NEED TO ORGANIZE AND FIND PROTECTION.

LET'S GET IT TOGETHER, FOLKS!

THEY WILL DECIDE THAT IT WOULD BE BETTER FOR EVERYONE TO GIVE UP THE UNLIMITED RIGHT TO WHATEVER THEY CAN LAY THEIR HANDS ON.

I HEREBY RELINQUISH MY RIGHT TO KILL YOU.

AND I YOU.

AND THEY WILL AGREE TO INSTITUTE A SOVEREIGN TO IMPOSE SOME ORDER ON AN ANARCHIC STATE OF AFFAIRS.

LET'S MAKE HIM OUR KING!

WOO!

YEAH!

THE SOVEREIGN WILL HAVE THE ABSOLUTE POWER TO MAKE LAWS AND COMPEL PEOPLE TO OBEY THEM.

WHAT DO I DO?

THE BEST KIND OF SOVEREIGNTY IS MONARCHY, SINCE ALL LAWS COME FROM ONE PERSON AND ALL POWER IS INVESTED IN A SINGLE AUTHORITY.

THIS "COVENANT" TO SET UP A POLITY WITH A SOVEREIGN AS HEAD IS MADE SOLELY BY THE PEOPLE.

THE DIVINE RIGHT OF KINGS?

NONSENSE!

SMACK!

A LEGITIMATE SOVEREIGN IS EMPOWERED BY THE CITIZENS WHO AUTHORIZE HIM, NOT BY GOD.

HOBBES'S ABSOLUTE SOVEREIGN GOVERNS ALL AFFAIRS OF STATE.

MY WORD IS LAW.

NO ONE HAS THE RIGHT TO DISOBEY THE SOVEREIGN, NO MATTER HOW MUCH THEY DISLIKE THE LAWS.

IMPRISONMENT FOR THIEVERY AND VIOLENCE!

AND THEY *WILL* OBEY, OUT OF FEAR. THE ALTERNATIVE WOULD BE A RETURN TO THE STATE OF NATURE. AND NO ONE WANTS THAT.

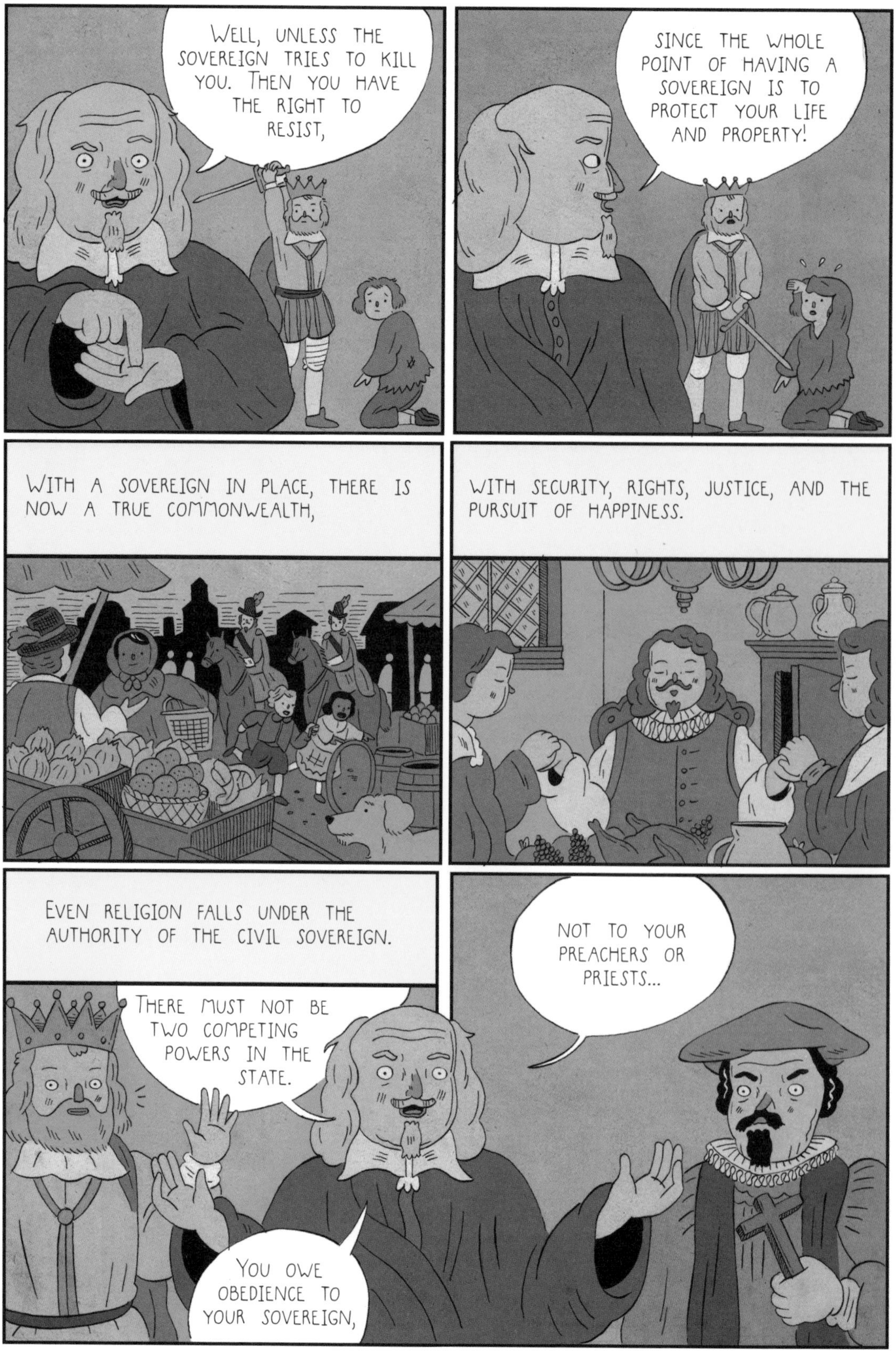

WELL, UNLESS THE SOVEREIGN TRIES TO KILL YOU. THEN YOU HAVE THE RIGHT TO RESIST,
SINCE THE WHOLE POINT OF HAVING A SOVEREIGN IS TO PROTECT YOUR LIFE AND PROPERTY!
WITH A SOVEREIGN IN PLACE, THERE IS NOW A TRUE COMMONWEALTH,
WITH SECURITY, RIGHTS, JUSTICE, AND THE PURSUIT OF HAPPINESS.
EVEN RELIGION FALLS UNDER THE AUTHORITY OF THE CIVIL SOVEREIGN.
THERE MUST NOT BE TWO COMPETING POWERS IN THE STATE.
YOU OWE OBEDIENCE TO YOUR SOVEREIGN,
NOT TO YOUR PREACHERS OR PRIESTS...

...AND DEFINITELY NOT TO SOME GUY IN ROME!

Ow!

HOBBES HAD SOME ESPECIALLY UNKIND THINGS TO SAY ABOUT CATHOLICISM.

GET OUT OF HERE!

HE DISCUSSES IT IN THE FINAL CHAPTERS OF *LEVIATHAN*, FOR WHICH HE HAD A SPECIAL TITLE.

"THE KINGDOM OF DARKNESS"!!

The Kingdom of Darkness

THE CIVIL SOVEREIGN, AS HEAD OF HIS COMMONWEALTH'S CHURCH, WILL ALONE DETERMINE WHAT COUNTS AS HOLY SCRIPTURE...

HMM...

AS WELL AS WHO IS PERMITTED TO INTERPRET THESE SACRED WRITINGS FOR THE PEOPLE...

HMM...

...AND EVEN WHAT IS OR IS NOT A MIRACLE.

IF THE SOVEREIGN SAYS IT IS SO, THEN NO CITIZEN MAY CONTRADICT IT.

IT'S A MIRACLE!

As for Hobbes's own religious beliefs, these are not entirely clear.

THERE ARE NO INCORPOREAL SUBSTANCES. GOD WOULD HAVE TO BE A BODY.

Hobbes's *LEVIATHAN* was a bold and radical effort to reveal the contractual and secular foundations of political authority,

Demonstrate the importance of absolute obedience to the civil sovereign,

And severely limit ecclesiastic power.

HEY GUYS, I'M OVER HERE!

The Englishman was not one to mince words, and his treatise was widely condemned as a dangerous book filled with "Godless" ideas.

IT WILL CORRUPT THE SOULS OF READERS!

But even Hobbes was astounded at what he read some years later in a new book by an excommunicated Jew living in Holland.

THE HAGUE

1670

BENTO (OR BARUCH) DE SPINOZA WAS BORN AND RAISED IN AMSTERDAM. HIS FAMILY BELONGED TO THAT CITY'S PORTUGUESE-JEWISH COMMUNITY.

THESE SEPHARDIC JEWS WERE DESCENDANTS OF GENERATIONS OF JEWS IN SPAIN AND PORTUGAL WHO, IN THE LATE 15TH CENTURY, HAD BEEN FORCED TO CONVERT TO CHRISTIANITY.

THE "CONVERSOS" SUFFERED UNDER THE SPANISH INQUISITION.

THEY MUST STILL BE PRACTICING JUDAISM IN SECRET!

MANY EVENTUALLY MIGRATED TO THE DUTCH REPUBLIC AT THE BEGINNING OF THE 17TH CENTURY.

THEY CAN SETTLE HERE AND PRACTICE THEIR JUDAISM.

THEY'LL BE GOOD FOR OUR ECONOMY!

AFTER HIS FATHER'S DEATH, AND WHILE STILL A YOUNG MAN, SPINOZA TOOK OVER THE FAMILY IMPORTING BUSINESS.

HE CONTINUED HIS STUDIES, HOWEVER, AND APPARENTLY REMAINED AN UPSTANDING MEMBER OF THE CONGREGATION.

BUT SUDDENLY, IN JULY OF 1656, THE TWENTY-THREE YEAR OLD SPINOZA WAS PERMANENTLY BANISHED FROM AMSTERDAM'S PORTUGUESE-JEWISH COMMUNITY,

WE EXCOMMUNICATE, CURSE, AND DAMN BARUCH DE SPINOZA. HE IS HEREBY EXPELLED FROM THE PEOPLE OF ISRAEL.

WITH GREAT PREJUDICE.

THE *HEREM* DOCUMENT SPEAKS OF HIS "ABOMINABLE HERESIES AND MONSTROUS DEEDS",

YOU ARE A MONSTER!

BUT DOES NOT MENTION WHAT THEY ARE.

CURSED BE HE BY DAY,

CURSED BE HE BY NIGHT.

SPINOZA HAD LOST HIS COMMITMENT TO THE JEWISH FAITH BY THIS POINT, AND SEEMS TO HAVE TAKEN IT ALL IN GOOD STRIDE.

ADEUS.

IN THE 1660S, SPINOZA SUPPORTED HIMSELF BY LENS-GRINDING...

AND WORKED ON HIS PHILOSOPHICAL MASTERPIECE, THE *ETHICS*.

HIS IDEAS ON GOD, MORALITY, AND RELIGION WERE EXTREMELY RADICAL – AND, IN THE EYES OF CONTEMPORARIES, HIGHLY DISTURBING.

ACCORDING TO SPINOZA, THERE IS NO SUCH THING AS A TRANSCENDENT, PROVIDENTIAL GOD – THE SUPERNATURAL AGENT OF THE ABRAHAMIC RELIGIONS.

GOD IS NATURE.

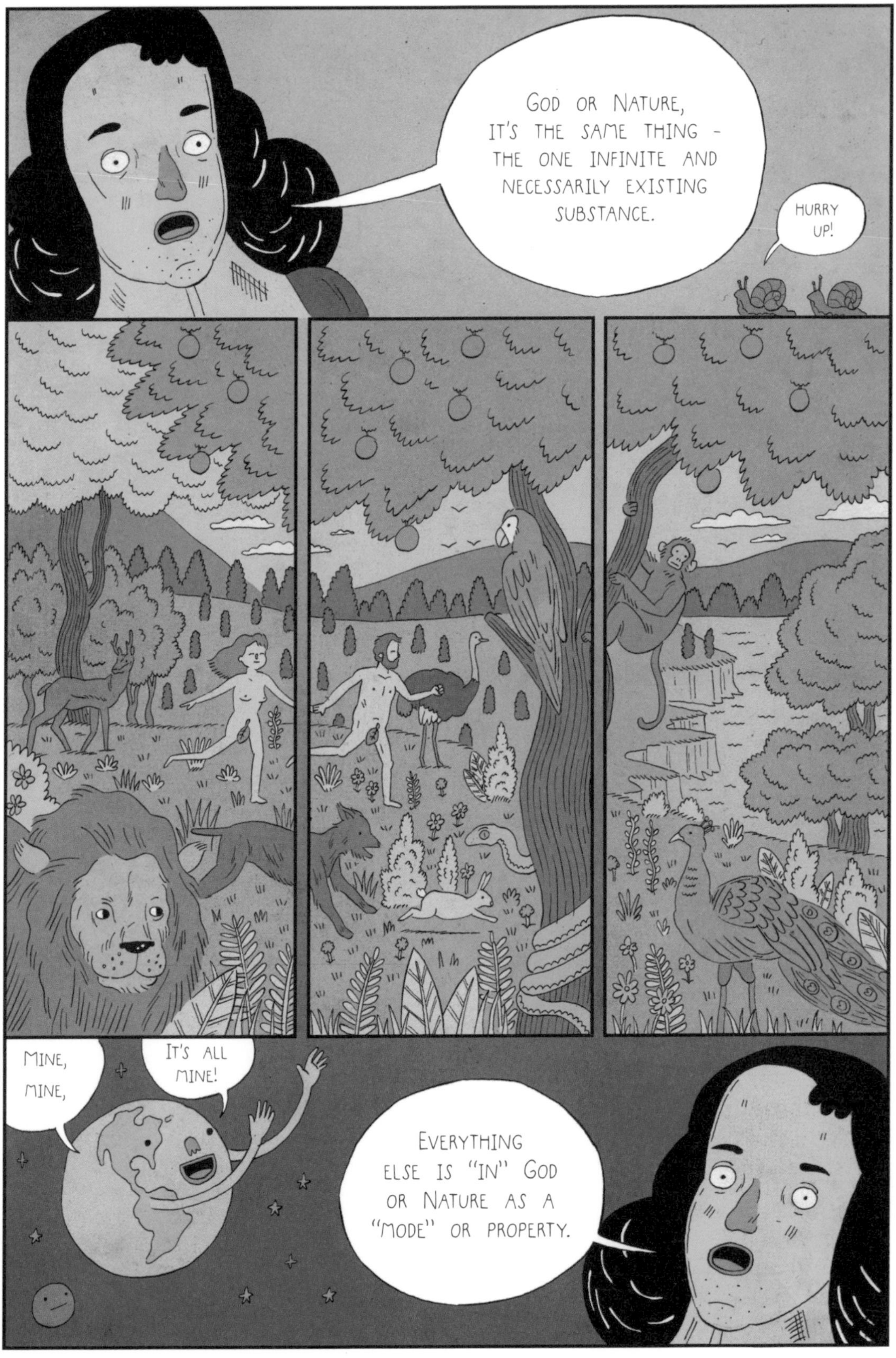
GOD OR NATURE, IT'S THE SAME THING - THE ONE INFINITE AND NECESSARILY EXISTING SUBSTANCE.
HURRY UP!
MINE, MINE,
IT'S ALL MINE!
EVERYTHING ELSE IS "IN" GOD OR NATURE AS A "MODE" OR PROPERTY.

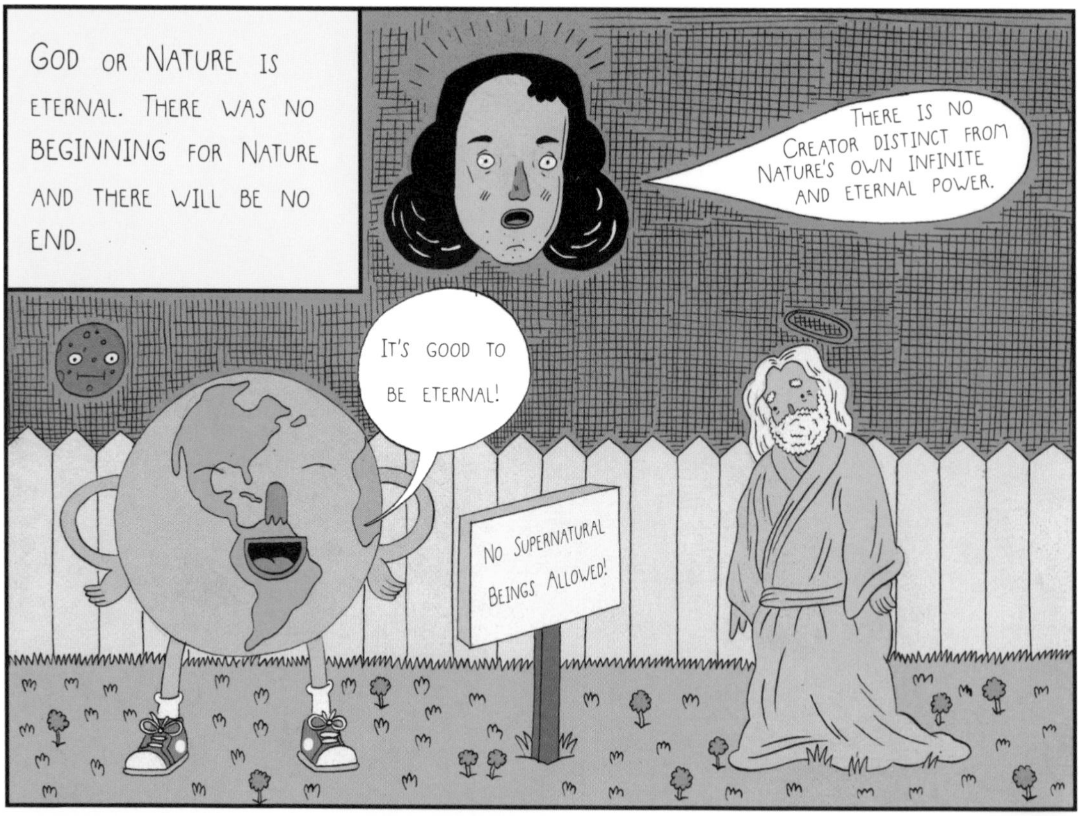
GOD OR NATURE IS ETERNAL. THERE WAS NO BEGINNING FOR NATURE AND THERE WILL BE NO END.
THERE IS NO CREATOR DISTINCT FROM NATURE'S OWN INFINITE AND ETERNAL POWER.
IT'S GOOD TO BE ETERNAL!
NO SUPERNATURAL BEINGS ALLOWED!

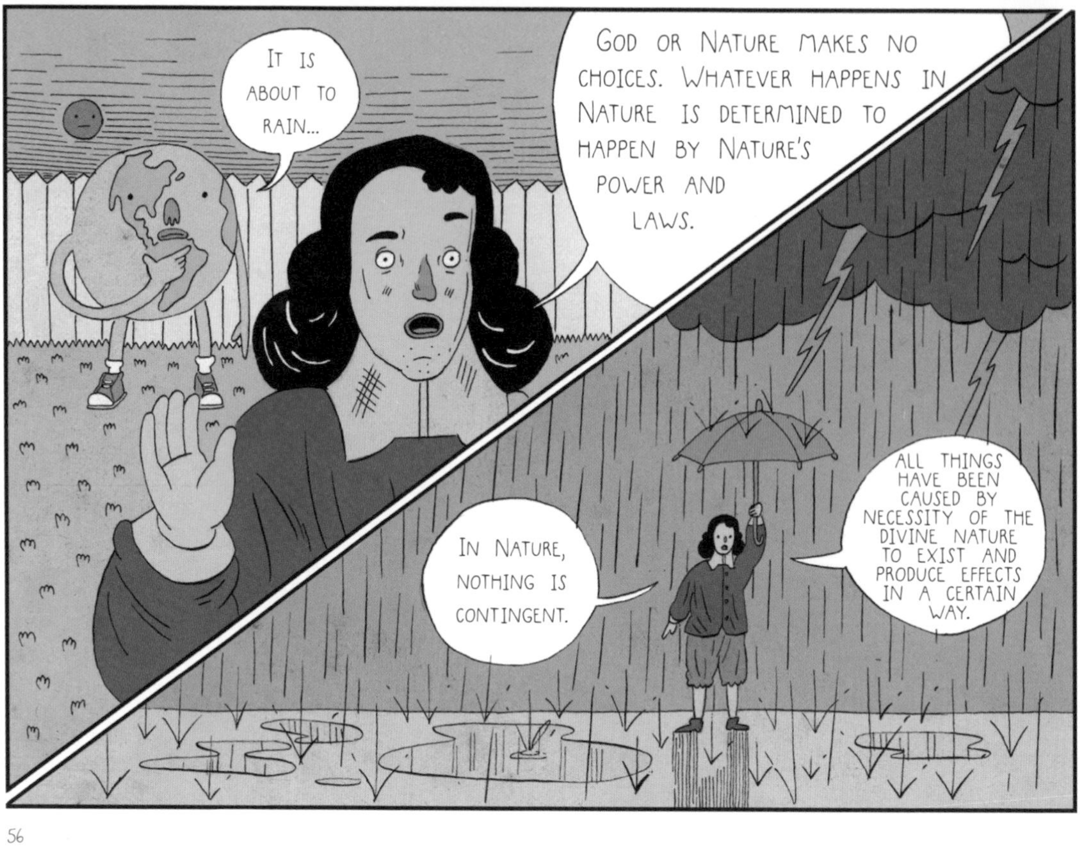
IT IS ABOUT TO RAIN...
GOD OR NATURE MAKES NO CHOICES. WHATEVER HAPPENS IN NATURE IS DETERMINED TO HAPPEN BY NATURE'S POWER AND LAWS.
IN NATURE, NOTHING IS CONTINGENT.
ALL THINGS HAVE BEEN CAUSED BY NECESSITY OF THE DIVINE NATURE TO EXIST AND PRODUCE EFFECTS IN A CERTAIN WAY.

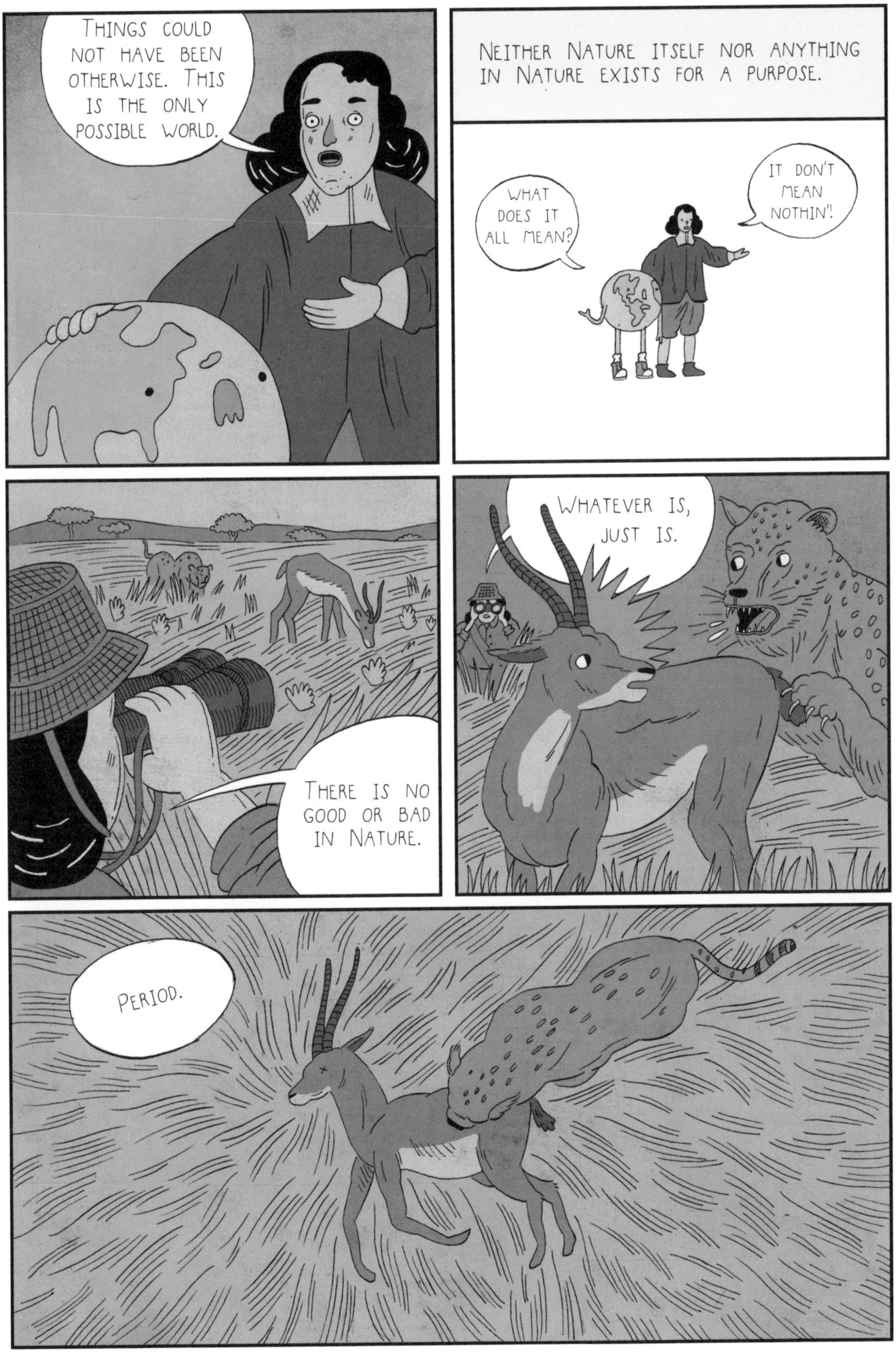
THINGS COULD NOT HAVE BEEN OTHERWISE. THIS IS THE ONLY POSSIBLE WORLD.
NEITHER NATURE ITSELF NOR ANYTHING IN NATURE EXISTS FOR A PURPOSE.
WHAT DOES IT ALL MEAN?
IT DON'T MEAN NOTHIN'!
THERE IS NO GOOD OR BAD IN NATURE.
WHATEVER IS, JUST IS.
PERIOD.

SPINOZA INSISTS THAT HUMAN BEINGS ARE AS MUCH A PART OF NATURE - AND SUBJECT TO ITS LAWS - AS ANYTHING ELSE.

WE ARE NOT SO SPECIAL. WE ARE NOT SOME KINGDOM UNTO OURSELVES.

WHATEVER IS TRUE OF US IS TRUE OF EVERYTHING IN NATURE.

OW!

THE THOUGHTS, DESIRES, EMOTIONS, AND CHOICES OF HUMAN BEINGS ARE ALL DETERMINED BY CAUSES.

THERE IS NO SUCH THING AS FREE WILL.

SPINOZA WAS STRONGLY INFLUENCED BY DESCARTES. BUT HE DISAGREED WITH THE DUALIST PICTURE OF MIND AND BODY.

MY MIND AND BODY ARE ONE AND THE SAME THING.

BUT EXPRESSED IN TWO DIFFERENT WAYS!

THE HUMAN BODY, LIKE ANY BODY, IS A MODE OF NATURE UNDER THE ATTRIBUTE OF EXTENSION - IT IS A PART OF NATURE'S MATERIAL REALM.

THE HUMAN MIND IS A MODE OF NATURE UNDER THE ATTRIBUTE OF THOUGHT - IT BELONGS TO NATURE'S MENTAL REALM.

THESE ATTRIBUTES OF NATURE ARE DISTINCT.

MINDS DO NOT CAUSE THINGS TO HAPPEN IN BODIES.

ONLY BODIES CAUSE MOTION IN OTHER BODIES.

HEY!

NOR DO BODIES CAUSE THINGS TO HAPPEN IN MINDS.

IDEAS OR THOUGHTS ARE AFFECTED ONLY BY OTHER IDEAS OR THOUGHTS.

HUH?

A HUMAN MIND IS NOTHING BUT A PARTICULAR ITEM IN NATURE'S MENTAL REALM THAT DIRECTLY CORRESPONDS TO A PARTICULAR BODY IN THE MATERIAL REALM.

THEY ARE, IN FACT, ONE AND THE SAME THING IN NATURE EXPRESSING ITSELF AS A BODY IN THE MATERIAL REALM AND AS A MIND IN THE MENTAL REALM.

A PAIN FELT IN THE MIND IS NOT *CAUSED* BY SOMETHING HAPPENING IN THE BODY. RATHER, IT IS SIMPLY THE EXPRESSION UNDER THE ATTRIBUTE OF THOUGHT

@#$*%!

CRUNCH!

OF THE SAME THING THAT IS EXPRESSING ITSELF UNDER THE ATTRIBUTE OF EXTENSION AS THE BODY'S PHYSICAL DISTRESS.

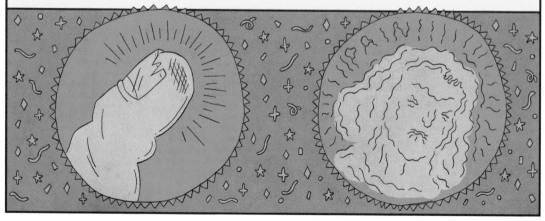

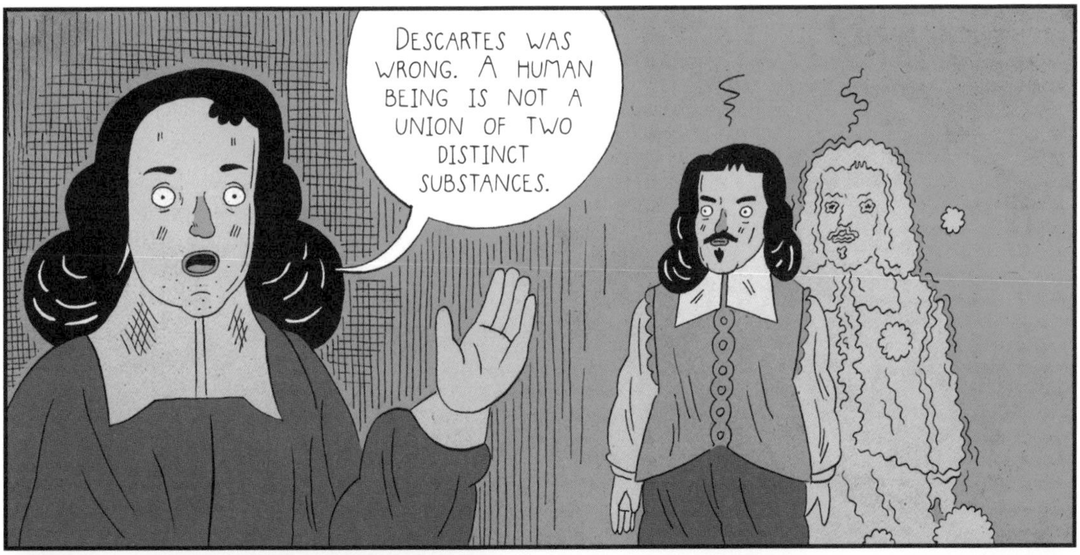
DESCARTES WAS WRONG. A HUMAN BEING IS NOT A UNION OF TWO DISTINCT SUBSTANCES.

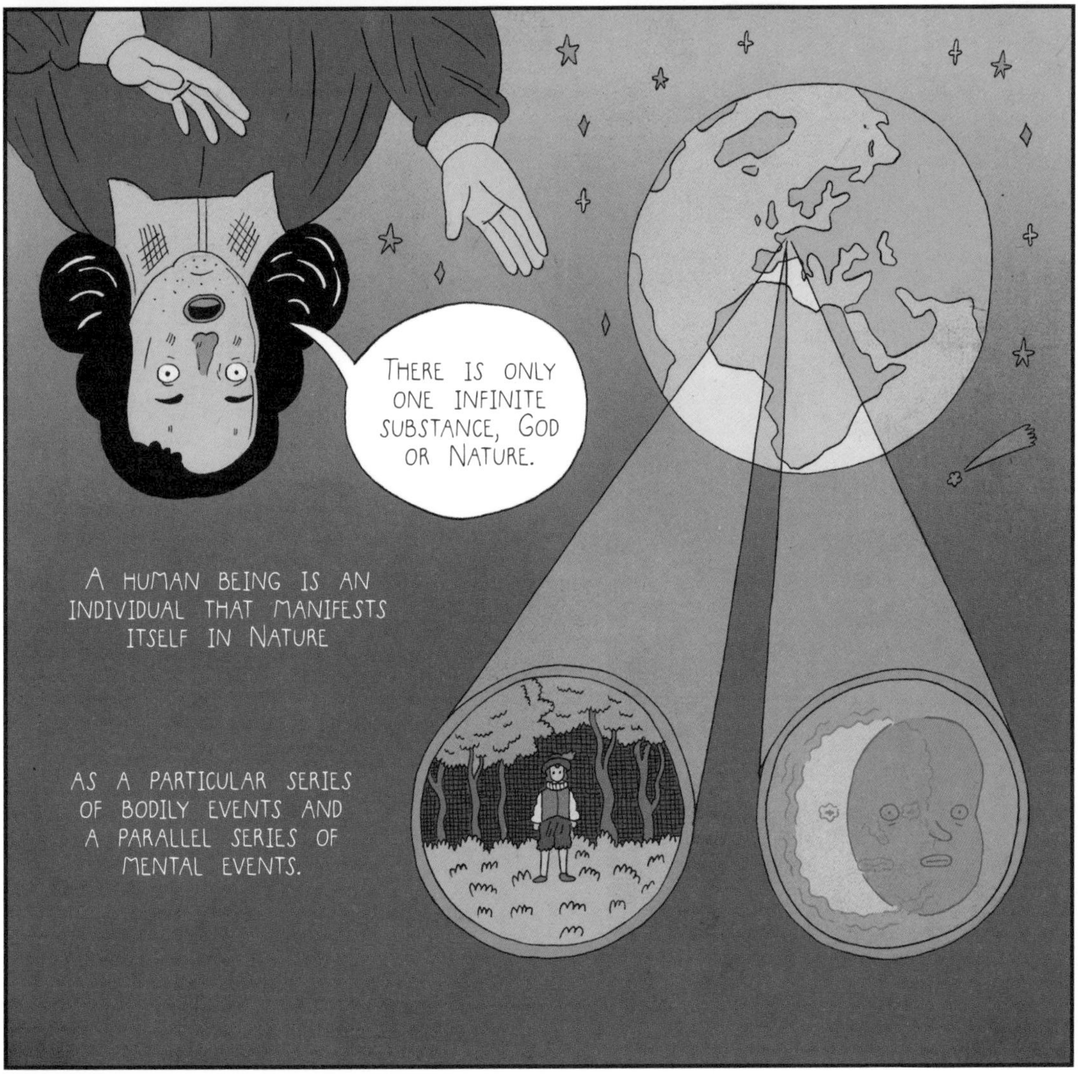
THERE IS ONLY ONE INFINITE SUBSTANCE, GOD OR NATURE.
A HUMAN BEING IS AN INDIVIDUAL THAT MANIFESTS ITSELF IN NATURE
AS A PARTICULAR SERIES OF BODILY EVENTS AND A PARALLEL SERIES OF MENTAL EVENTS.

SPINOZA'S METAPHYSICAL EXPLANATION OF WHAT WE ARE AND HOW WE ARE A PART OF NATURE LAYS THE FOUNDATIONS FOR HIS ACCOUNT OF HOW WE LIVE — AND SHOULD LIVE — OUR LIVES.

IT ALL DEPENDS ON WHAT CAUSES ARE DETERMINING OUR CHOICES AND ACTIONS.

ARE WE GUIDED BY OUR PASSIONS, BY THE WAYS IN WHICH WE ARE MADE TO FEEL BY THINGS IN THE WORLD AS THEY AFFECT US?

BURP!

GUY'S NIGHT!

OR DO WE LEAD OURSELVES THROUGH REASON, BY WHAT WE KNOW TO BE TRUE AND IN OUR BEST INTEREST?

ACTUALLY, I SHOULD GET TO BED.

DO WE PASSIVELY SUFFER THE SLINGS AND ARROWS OF OUTRAGEOUS FORTUNE?

OR ARE WE ACTIVE AND IN CONTROL OF OUR LIVES?

LET'S FIND SOMETHING BETTER TO DO.

WE'RE TAKING CONTROL OF OUR LIVES.

THANKS ANYWAYS!

A LIFE GOVERNED BY THE PASSIONS IS A LIFE OF BONDAGE. A PERSON IS A SLAVE TO HIS DESIRES FOR THINGS NOT UNDER HIS CONTROL.

HIS HAPPINESS IS SUBJECT TO GOOD LUCK AND BAD LUCK.

POOF!

WHAT IS ESPECIALLY TROUBLING

IS THE BELIEF IN A PROVIDENTIAL GOD.

TO THINK THAT GOD IS A PERSONAL AGENT WHO WILL DISPENSE ETERNAL REWARD AND PUNISHMENT MEANS THAT YOUR LIFE WILL BE DIRECTED NOT BY KNOWLEDGE BUT BY THE EMOTIONS OF HOPE AND FEAR.

ON THE OTHER HAND, A LIFE UNDER THE GUIDANCE OF REASON —

WILL BE A LIFE OF FREEDOM, VIRTUE, AND PEACE OF MIND.

ESPECIALLY AN UNDERSTANDING OF HOW ALL THINGS, INCLUDING OURSELVES, ARE A PART OF NATURE AND NECESSITATED BY ITS LAWS —

WE WILL BEAR CALMLY THOSE THINGS THAT HAPPEN TO US CONTRARY TO OUR WELL-BEING,

OW!

WHEN WE REALIZE THAT WE COULD NOT HAVE AVOIDED THEM AND THAT WE, NO LESS THAN OTHER THINGS, MUST FOLLOW NATURE'S ORDER.

THE TRULY FREE PERSON WILL KNOW THAT THERE IS NO SUCH THING AS FREE WILL OR AN IMMORTAL SOUL, AND SO SHE WILL NOT BE TROUBLED BY IRRATIONAL BELIEFS ABOUT AN AFTERLIFE.

A FREE PERSON THINKS LEAST OF ALL OF DEATH.

THE REWARDS OF THE LIFE OF REASON AND VIRTUE ARE IN *THIS* WORLD.

HAPPINESS!

WELL-BEING!

KNOWLEDGE!

IN THE LATE 1660s, WITH THE LIBERAL AND TOLERANT IDEALS OF HOLLAND UNDER ASSAULT BY POLITICAL CONSERVATIVES AND THEIR RELIGIOUS ALLIES,

SPINOZA PUT ASIDE THE *ETHICS* TO COMPOSE HIS *THEOLOGICAL-POLITICAL TREATISE.*

IN THE *TREATISE*, SPINOZA ARGUES THAT POLITICAL STABILITY AND SOCIAL WELL-BEING REQUIRE:

DEMOCRACY...

INTELLECTUAL FREEDOM...

AND A CIVIL GOVERNMENT

WHAM!

FREE OF ECCLESIASTICAL INTERFERENCE.

THE FREEDOM OF PHILOSOPHIZING IS ESSENTIAL FOR THE PEACE AND PIETY OF THE REPUBLIC!

He makes his case by showing that the Bible, which religious leaders use to influence the hearts and minds of citizens, was not literally written by God.

Its authors were ordinary human beings addressing very particular historical circumstances.

Scripture consists of different books written at different times for different audiences by different authors.

The original texts were copied many times and handed down through the centuries...

And finally edited into a single collection long after they had been written.

HOLY SCRIPTURE

The text of the Bible as we have it is a corrupt and mutilated work of human literature.

What makes the Bible "divine" is only its morally edifying influence upon readers.

The divinity of Scripture lies solely in the fact that it teaches true virtue.

THE PROPHETS WHO WROTE THESE BOOKS WERE NOT PHILOSOPHERS OR SCIENTISTS OR EVEN THEOLOGIANS.

WHAT THE...?

AND SO WHAT THEY SAY ABOUT GOD, NATURE, AND HUMAN BEINGS IS NOT NECESSARILY TRUE.

THIS LOOKS PRETTY MUCH RIGHT.

JOSHUA WAS NOT AN ASTRONOMER; HE REALLY BELIEVED THE SUN WENT AROUND THE EARTH.

THE PROPHETS WERE, HOWEVER, MEN OF EXTRAORDINARY VIRTUE AND VIVID IMAGINATION.

THEIR MESSAGE, ELOQUENTLY TOLD, IS A SIMPLE ONE.

LOVE YOUR NEIGHBOR!

TRUE RELIGION CONSISTS ONLY IN JUSTICE AND CHARITY TOWARD OTHERS.

EVERYTHING ELSE - ALL THE CEREMONIES AND RITES OF ORGANIZED RELIGIONS - HAS NOTHING TO DO WITH PIETY.

RELIGION HAS DEGENERATED INTO PERNICIOUS SUPERSTITION.

SPINOZA ALSO ARGUES THAT MIRACLES ARE IMPOSSIBLE.

GOD *IS* NATURE, AND NOTHING CAN HAPPEN IN NATURE THAT CONTRAVENES ITS OWN UNIVERSAL LAWS.

WHOA!

WHAT WE CALL A "MIRACLE" IS ONLY AN EVENT WHOSE NATURAL CAUSE WE HAVE NOT YET DISCOVERED.

SPINOZA IS, ABOVE ALL, CONCERNED TO SHOW THAT LIBERTY OF THOUGHT AND EXPRESSION IS ESSENTIAL TO THE WELL-BEING OF A POLITY.

IN A FREE COMMONWEALTH, EVERYONE MAY THINK AS HE PLEASES AND SAY WHAT HE THINKS.

HEY!

ANY EFFORTS TO REPRESS INTELLECTUAL FREEDOM IN THE NAME OF RELIGION WILL ONLY BACKFIRE AND BE HARMFUL TO SOCIETY.

IT IS UP TO THE CIVIL AUTHORITIES, NOT RELIGIOUS LEADERS, TO GOVERN THE LIVES OF CITIZENS.

SCREEEECH!

THUS SPINOZA, LIKE HOBBES, SAYS THAT EVEN RELIGIOUS AFFAIRS ARE TO BE OVERSEEN BY SECULAR AUTHORITIES.

IT IS DISASTROUS FOR BOTH RELIGION AND STATE TO ALLOW RELIGIOUS FUNCTIONARIES THE RIGHT TO MEDDLE IN STATE BUSINESS.

UNLIKE HOBBES, HOWEVER, SPINOZA INSISTS THAT DEMOCRACY IS THE BEST POLITICAL SYSTEM FOR INSURING PEACE AND PROGRESS.

IT APPROACHES MOST CLOSELY THAT FREEDOM THAT NATURE GRANTS TO EVERY PERSON.

SPINOZA'S *THEOLOGICAL-POLITICAL TREATISE* WAS PUBLISHED ANONYMOUSLY IN 1670, WITH A FALSE PUBLISHER AND CITY ON THE TITLE PAGE AS A PRECAUTION.

THESE ARE DANGEROUS TIMES, ESPECIALLY FOR SOMEONE WHO SPEAKS HIS MIND!

THE BOOK CAUSED A TREMENDOUS UPROAR AND A VICIOUS BACKLASH.

THIS IS AN EVIL, ATHEISTIC TREATISE THAT WILL CORRUPT THE SOULS OF READERS!

THE *TREATISE* WAS ATTACKED BY RELIGIOUS AUTHORITIES AND BANNED BY CIVIC BODIES IN HOLLAND AND ELSEWHERE.

ONE CRITIC LABELED IT "A BOOK FORGED IN HELL BY THE DEVIL HIMSELF".

EVEN THOMAS HOBBES WAS TAKEN ABACK BY SPINOZA'S AUDACITY.

I DURST NOT WRITE SO BOLDLY!

IN THE SPRING OF 1676, A MYSTERIOUS VISITOR CAME TO SEE SPINOZA IN THE HAGUE.

HE WAS GERMAN, AND SAID HE WAS A FELLOW PHILOSOPHER.

- OR WAS HE A SPY?

HE VERY MUCH WANTED TO MEET THE AUTHOR OF THE SCANDALOUS *THEOLOGICAL-POLITICAL TREATISE.*

HANOVER

1686

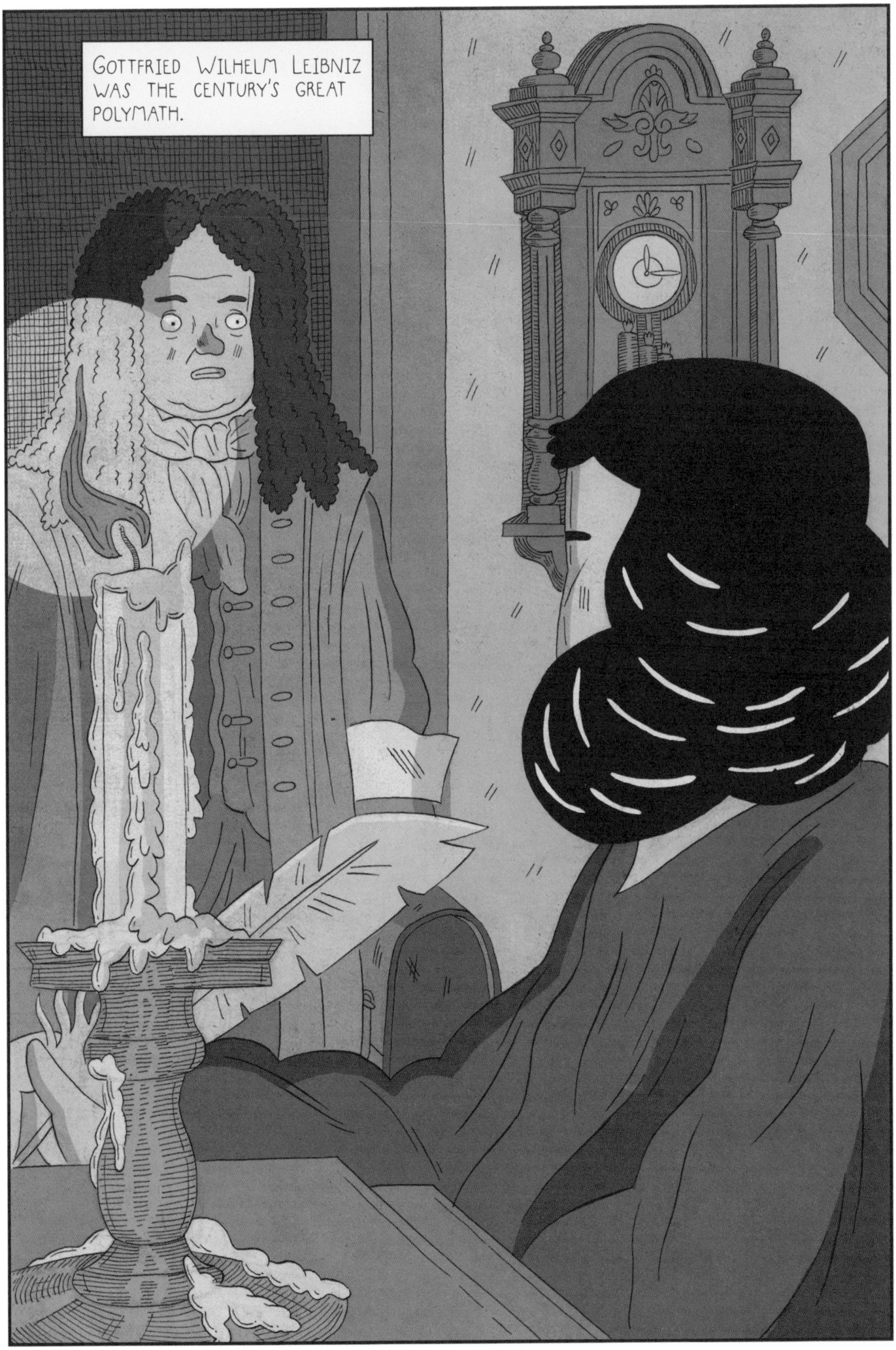
GOTTFRIED WILHELM LEIBNIZ WAS THE CENTURY'S GREAT POLYMATH.

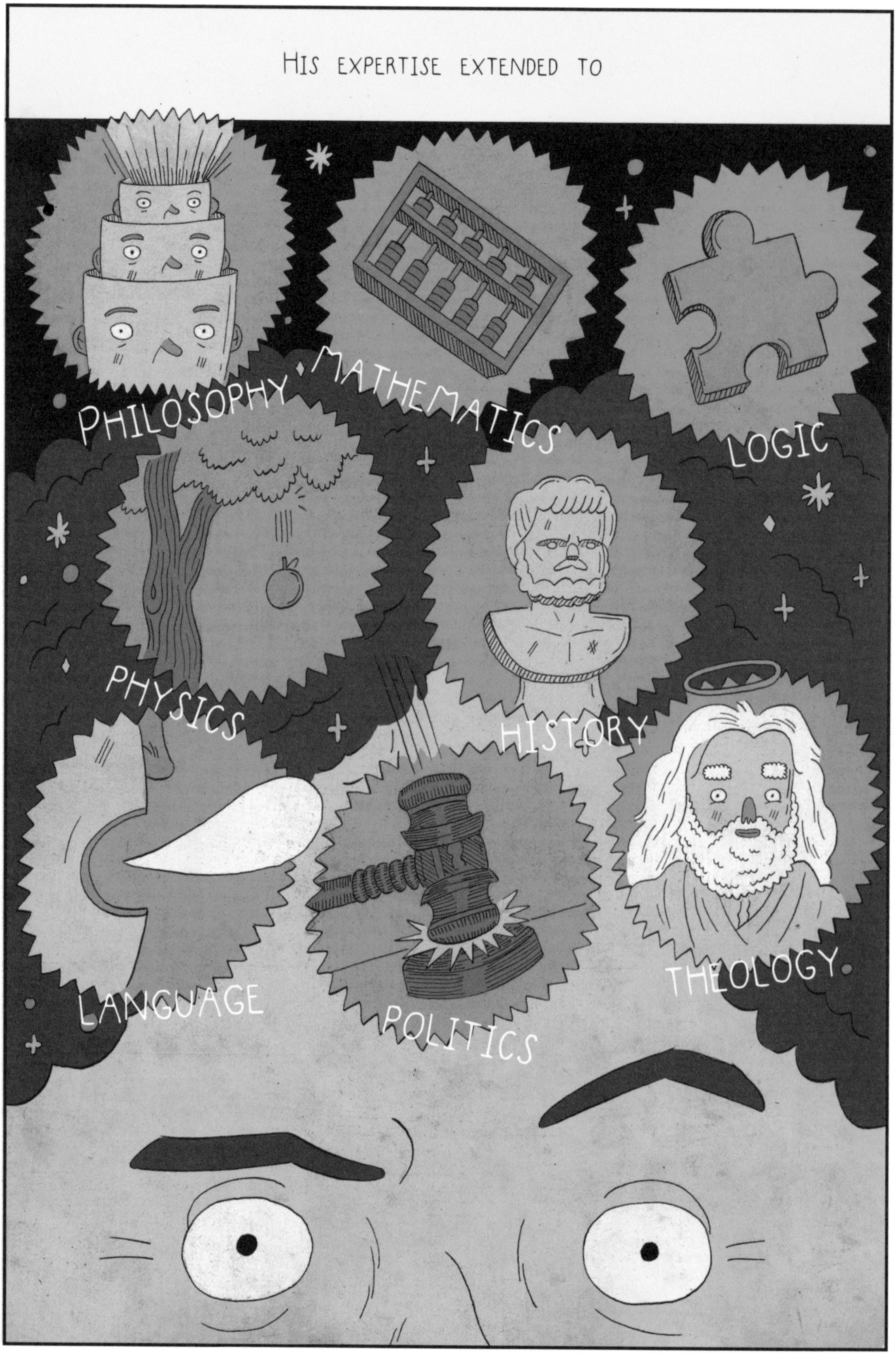
HIS EXPERTISE EXTENDED TO
PHILOSOPHY
MATHEMATICS
LOGIC
PHYSICS
HISTORY
LANGUAGE
POLITICS
THEOLOGY

He developed calculus, the mathematical study of change and infinitesimals.

Now wait a second! - It was I who discovered it. He copied me!

So *you* say, Newton!

(They probably both discovered it independently.)

He was also an inventor, and designed a calculating machine.

In the fall of 1676, Leibniz was on his way home after four years in Paris, where he had been sent on a diplomatic mission by the Elector of Mainz.

Don't tell my boss, but what I was really doing there was checking out the philosophical scene.

He took advantage of the return journey to make a detour to Holland and meet the infamous Spinoza.

LEIBNIZ, A LUTHERAN, AND *SPINOZA*, AN EXCOMMUNICATED JEW, MUST HAVE HAD QUITE A CONVERSATION.

LEIBNIZ KNEW SPINOZA'S VIEWS ON RELIGION, THE BIBLE, AND MIRACLES FROM THE *THEOLOGICAL-POLITICAL TREATISE*.

I'M SHOCKED! SHOCKED, I TELL YOU!!

BUT WHAT LEIBNIZ REALLY WANTED TO KNOW MORE ABOUT WAS SPINOZA'S METAPHYSICS.

TAKE A LOOK AT THE MANUSCRIPT OF MY *ETHICS*.

I MEAN, REALLY?! GOD AND NATURE ARE THE SAME THING?

YOU THINK THAT THINGS COULD NOT HAVE BEEN OTHERWISE?

THIS IS THE ONLY POSSIBLE WORLD?

LEIBNIZ WAS TROUBLED BY SPINOZA'S ACCOUNT OF THE NECESSITY OF THE WORLD AND EVERYTHING IN IT.

PROBABLY BECAUSE HIS OWN PHILOSOPHY SEEMED TO COME DANGEROUSLY CLOSE TO SUCH A CONCLUSION.

I'D BETTER BE CAREFUL HERE.

BY 1686, LEIBNIZ, NOW WORKING FOR THE DUKE OF HANOVER, HAD FIGURED OUT SOME METAPHYSICAL THINGS OF HIS OWN.

JUST A LITTLE SOMETHING I'VE PUT TOGETHER.

IN HIS *DISCOURSE ON METAPHYSICS*, HE INSISTS THAT THIS IS NOT THE ONLY POSSIBLE WORLD.

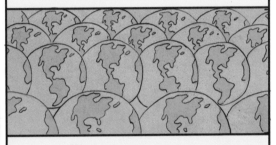

THERE ARE INFINITELY MANY POSSIBLE WORLDS THAT GOD COULD HAVE CREATED.

BUT THIS IS THE *BEST* OF ALL POSSIBLE WORLDS.

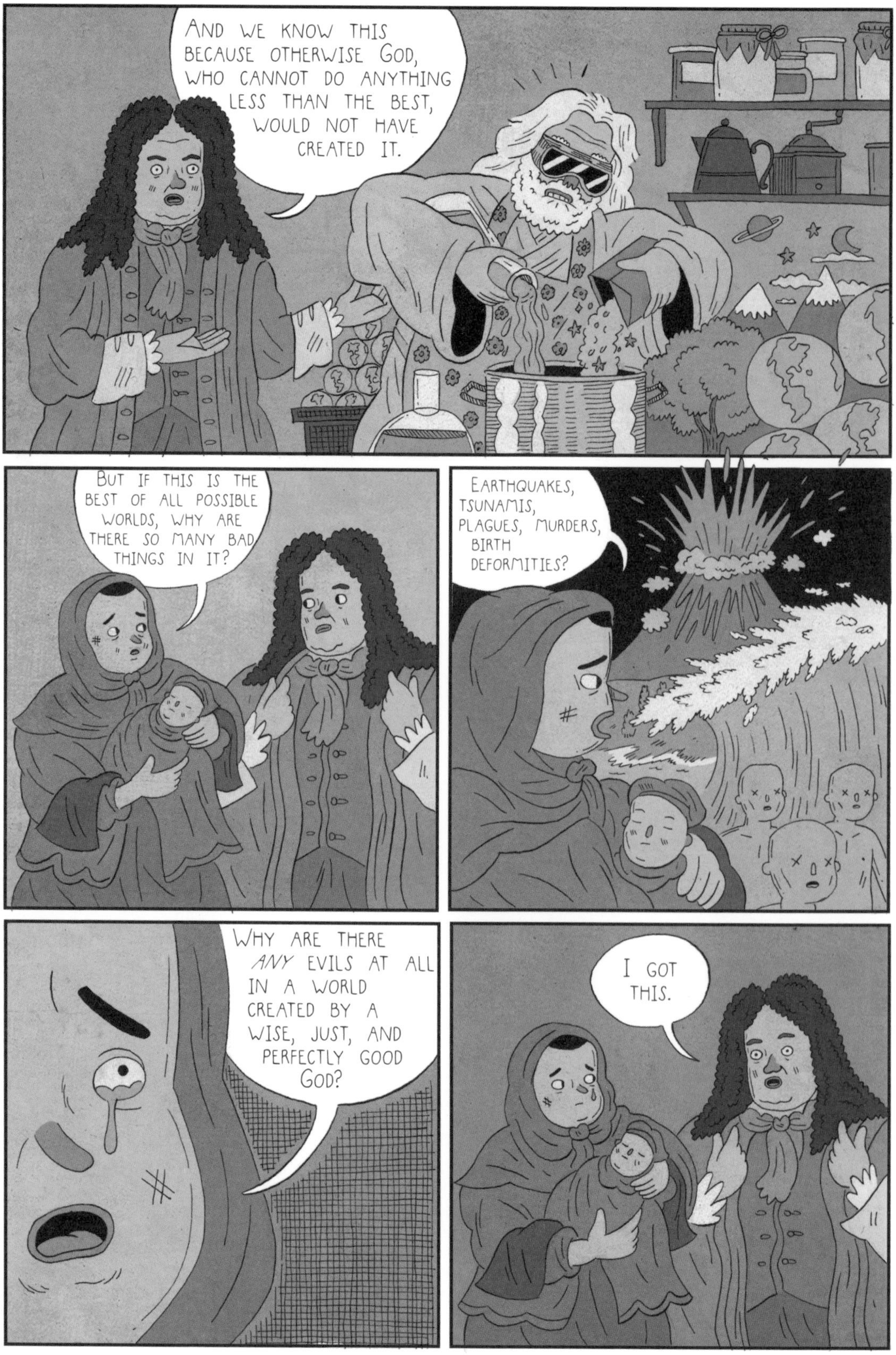
AND WE KNOW THIS BECAUSE OTHERWISE GOD, WHO CANNOT DO ANYTHING LESS THAN THE BEST, WOULD NOT HAVE CREATED IT.
BUT IF THIS IS THE BEST OF ALL POSSIBLE WORLDS, WHY ARE THERE SO MANY BAD THINGS IN IT?
EARTHQUAKES, TSUNAMIS, PLAGUES, MURDERS, BIRTH DEFORMITIES?
WHY ARE THERE *ANY* EVILS AT ALL IN A WORLD CREATED BY A WISE, JUST, AND PERFECTLY GOOD GOD?
I GOT THIS.

LEIBNIZ COINED THE TERM "THEODICY" FOR A SOLUTION TO THIS PHILOSOPHICAL CONUNDRUM.

YOU'RE LOOKING IN THE WRONG PLACE.

THE BESTNESS OF THE WORLD IS NOT SOMETHING YOU CAN SEE.

WHAT MAKES THIS WORLD THE BEST OF ALL POSSIBLE WORLDS IS THAT IT HAS THE SIMPLEST LAWS AND THE RICHEST PHENOMENA.

BEING THE BEST WORLD OVERALL DOES NOT MEAN THAT IT WILL BE BEST FOR EVERY INDIVIDUAL IN IT.

I'M AFRAID THAT IN THE BEST WORLD, THERE WILL BE SUFFERING. NOT EVERYONE WILL BE HAPPY.

AND IN PAINTING, WHERE SHADOWS ALLOW THE ILLUMINATED PARTS TO EMERGE...

AS IN MUSIC, WHERE DISSONANCE IS NECESSARY TO HIGHLIGHT THE HARMONY...

SO IN THE BEST WORLD THERE WILL BE DEFECTS THAT MAKE THE PERFECTIONS STAND OUT EVEN MORE CLEARLY.

A WORLD WITH EVEN ONE LESS NATURAL DISASTER OR ONE LESS SINNER WOULD NOT BE *THIS* WORLD, AND SO WOULD BE LESS THAN THE BEST AND NOT WORTHY OF GOD'S CHOICE.

GOD THUS *ALLOWS* THE EVILS TO HAPPEN, BUT DOES NOT DIRECTLY DESIRE THEM.

GOD'S CHOICE OF THIS WORLD WAS MOTIVATED, EVEN DETERMINED, BY WISDOM AND JUSTICE.

I SAID, "DETERMINED," NOT "NECESSITATED."

NEXT!

LEIBNIZ'S GOD MADE A CHOICE FOR A COMPELLING, EVEN IRRESISTIBLE REASON, BUT IT WAS STILL A *FREE* CHOICE.

WE'LL LET YOU KNOW.

FROM GOD'S CHOICE TO CREATE THIS WORLD, EVERYTHING ELSE — EVERY THING AND EVENT THAT IS A PART OF THIS WORLD — NECESSARILY FOLLOWS.

NOTHING HAPPENS WITHOUT A CAUSE OR REASON. WHATEVER HAPPENS HAS BEEN DETERMINED TO HAPPEN.

But because alternative possibilities are still *conceivable*, the necessity of things is not a logical or absolute necessity.

Adam and Eve chose to eat the fruit.

And given God's choice of this world with this Adam and this Eve,

They could not have done otherwise.

Still, they chose to eat it freely.

THIS world with *THIS* Adam and Eve eating *THIS* fruit is not the only logically possible world.

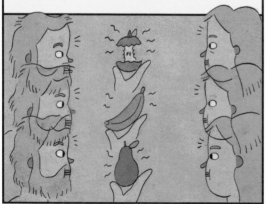

Other worlds with other Adams and other Eves are still possible "in themselves," although God would certainly *NOT* have chosen any of those worlds, since they are not compatible with divine wisdom.

Mom! I got the part!

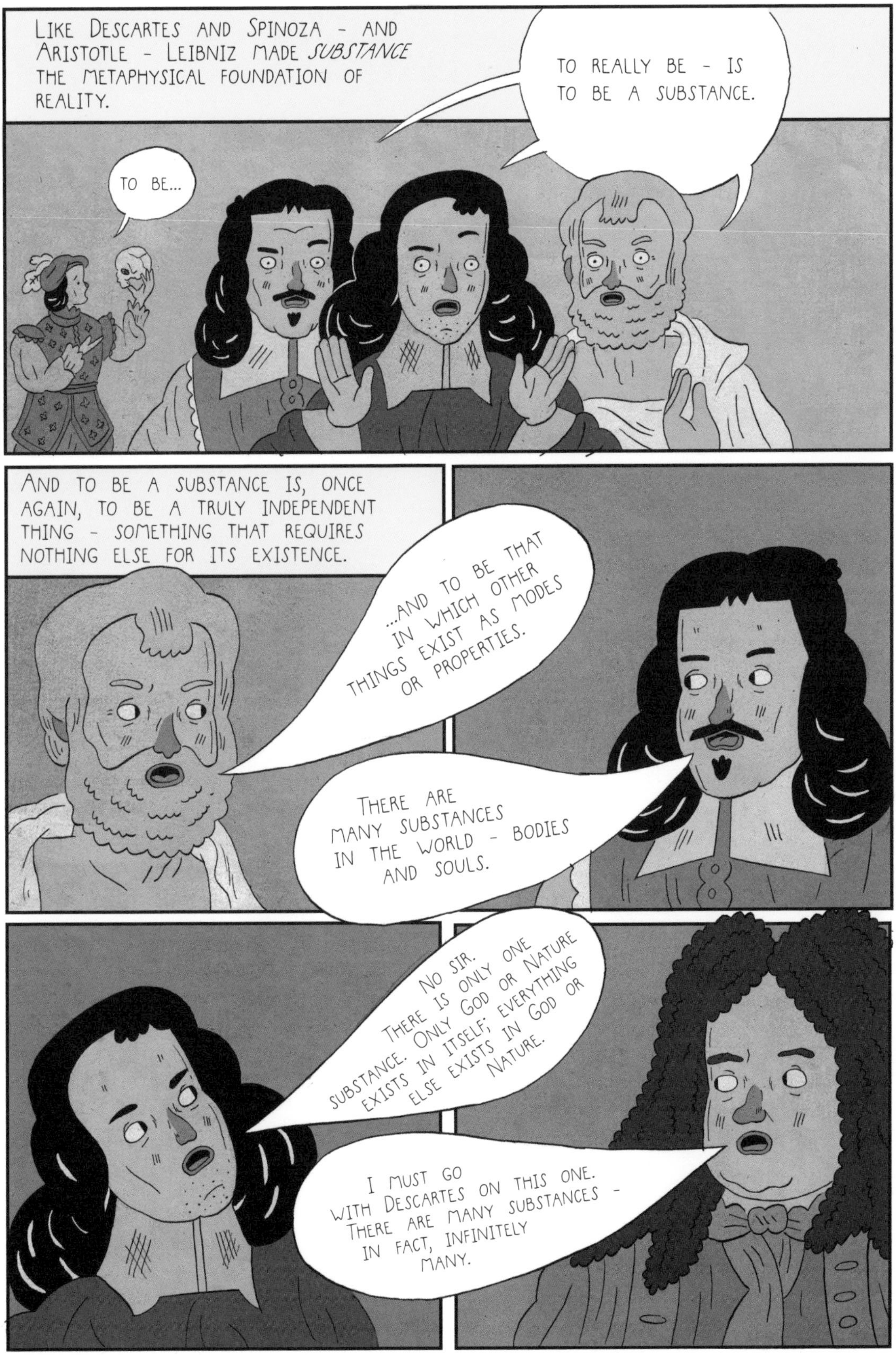
LIKE DESCARTES AND SPINOZA - AND ARISTOTLE - LEIBNIZ MADE *SUBSTANCE* THE METAPHYSICAL FOUNDATION OF REALITY.
TO BE...
TO REALLY BE - IS TO BE A SUBSTANCE.
AND TO BE A SUBSTANCE IS, ONCE AGAIN, TO BE A TRULY INDEPENDENT THING - SOMETHING THAT REQUIRES NOTHING ELSE FOR ITS EXISTENCE.
...AND TO BE THAT IN WHICH OTHER THINGS EXIST AS MODES OR PROPERTIES.
THERE ARE MANY SUBSTANCES IN THE WORLD - BODIES AND SOULS.
NO SIR. THERE IS ONLY ONE SUBSTANCE. ONLY GOD OR NATURE EXISTS IN ITSELF; EVERYTHING ELSE EXISTS IN GOD OR NATURE.
I MUST GO WITH DESCARTES ON THIS ONE. THERE ARE MANY SUBSTANCES - IN FACT, INFINITELY MANY.

I'M A SUBSTANCE.

YOU'RE A SUBSTANCE.

LIONS AND TIGERS AND BEARS ARE SUBSTANCES.

I'M OUTTA HERE!

BUT LEIBNIZ'S AGREEMENT WITH DESCARTES GOES ONLY SO FAR.

MY CONCEPT

IT IS OF THE NATURE OF AN INDIVIDUAL SUBSTANCE TO BE A COMPLETE BEING.

HE BELIEVED THAT INDEPENDENT EXISTENCE IMPLIES TOTAL SELF-SUFFICIENCY.

ITS CONCEPT ALONE MUST ALLOW FOR THE DEDUCTION OF ALL THE PROPERTIES THAT EVER PERTAIN TO THAT SUBSTANCE.

A SUBSTANCE CANNOT DEPEND IN ANY WAY - CAUSALLY OR OTHERWISE - ON ANYTHING ELSE.

OTHER THAN GOD, OF COURSE.

NOTHING THAT BELONGS TO OR HAPPENS TO A SUBSTANCE CAN COME FROM OUTSIDE IT.

A TRUE SUBSTANCE IS ACTIVE AND HAS PERFECT SPONTANEITY.

IT GENERATES ALL ITS OWN STATES AND ACTIONS THROUGH ITS NATURE ALONE.

AN INDIVIDUAL SUBSTANCE'S NATURE *DETERMINES* WHAT IT IS AND WHAT IT DOES.

ADAM EATS THE APPLE ONLY BECAUSE THIS ACT FOLLOWS FROM HIS NATURE.

BUT HE STILL EATS IT FREELY.

AND LET ME TELL YOU, IT'S A PRETTY GOOD APPLE!

AND THE SUBSTANCE AND ITS ACTIONS ARE ESSENTIAL FEATURES OF *THIS* WORLD.

ADAM EXISTS WITH THIS NATURE ONLY BECAUSE HE IS A PART OF THE BEST WORLD CHOSEN BY GOD.

LEIBNIZ CONCLUDES THAT IF ANY SUBSTANCE MUST BE THE ACTIVE SOURCE OF ITS OWN STATES, THERE CAN BE NO CAUSAL *INTERACTION* BETWEEN SUBSTANCES.

BUT WAIT! IT CERTAINLY LOOKS LIKE THINGS IN THE WORLD ARE INTERACTING AND CAUSING EFFECTS IN EACH OTHER.

I TELL A FRIEND TO MEET ME AT A CERTAIN PLACE, AND LO AND BEHOLD, THERE HE IS

AT THE RIGHT PLACE AT THE RIGHT TIME.

WHEN I SIT ON SOMETHING SHARP -

YOW!

AND MY BODY-SUBSTANCE SUFFERS A WOUND,

MY MIND-SUBSTANCE EXPERIENCES PAIN.

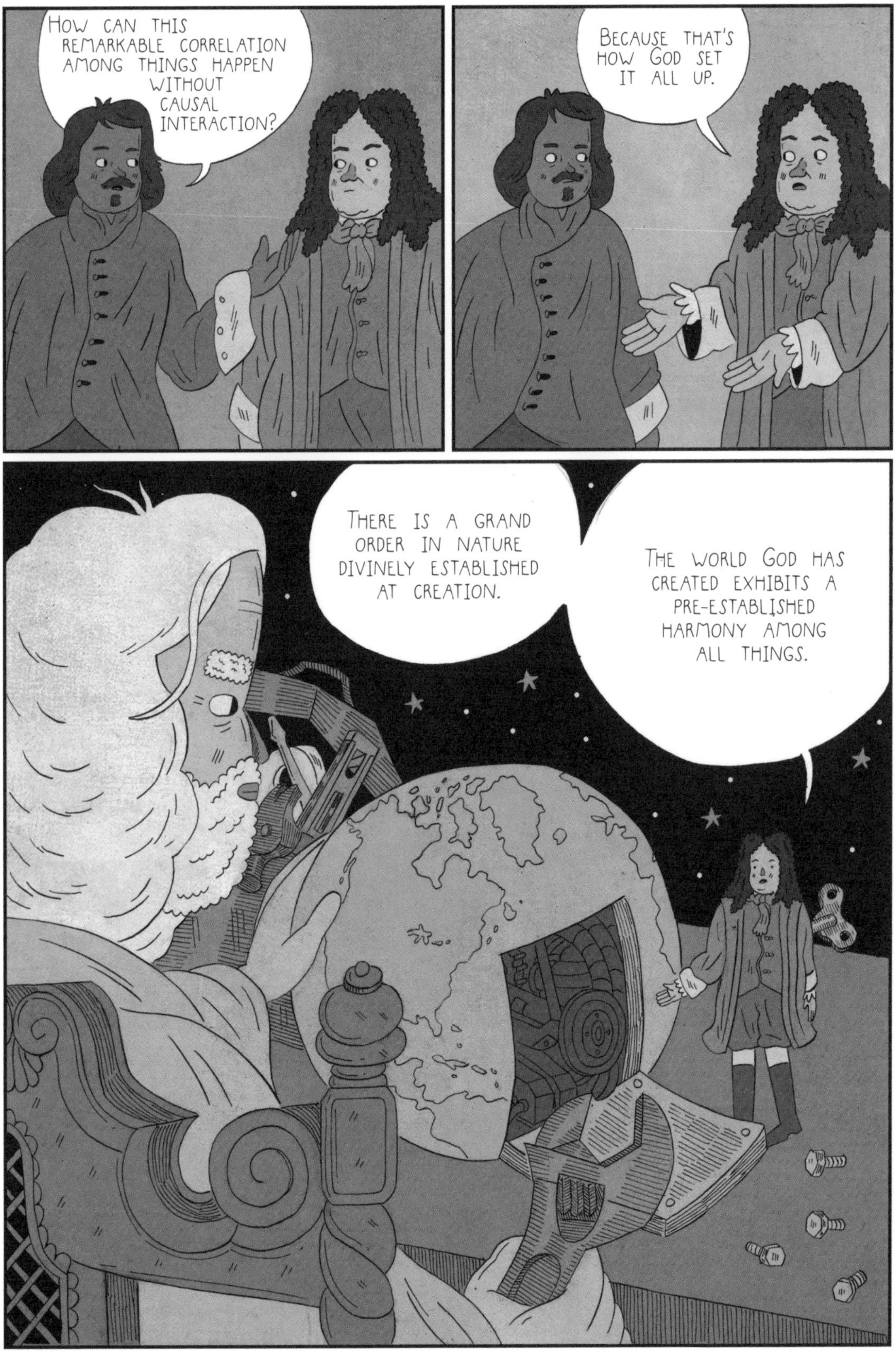
HOW CAN THIS REMARKABLE CORRELATION AMONG THINGS HAPPEN WITHOUT CAUSAL INTERACTION?
BECAUSE THAT'S HOW GOD SET IT ALL UP.
THERE IS A GRAND ORDER IN NATURE DIVINELY ESTABLISHED AT CREATION.
THE WORLD GOD HAS CREATED EXHIBITS A PRE-ESTABLISHED HARMONY AMONG ALL THINGS.

GOD HAS FORMED EACH OF THESE SUBSTANCES IN SUCH A WAY THAT EACH ONE, FOLLOWING ITS OWN LAWS, AGREES WITH ALL THE OTHERS,

AS IF THERE WERE A MUTUAL INFLUENCE, BUT WITHOUT THEIR ACTUALLY ACTING UPON ONE ANOTHER.

ACCORDING TO LEIBNIZ'S THEORY:

PRE-ESTABLISHED HARMONY.

THE STATES OF ALL SUBSTANCES FLOW FROM THEIR INDIVIDUAL NATURES SEPARATELY BUT IN A MAGNIFICENT, DIVINELY INSTITUTED CORRESPONDENCE WITH EACH OTHER.

IMAGINE THAT A CLOCKMAKER SETS TWO CLOCKS TO THE SAME TIME AND THEN WINDS THEM UP.

DING! DING! DING! DING!

WHEN ONE CLOCK STRIKES NOON, SO WILL THE OTHER. BUT THE FIRST CLOCK DOES NOT CAUSE THE SECOND CLOCK TO CHIME.

SO THE STATES OF THE MIND AND THE STATES OF THE BODY IN A HUMAN BEING UNFOLD, EACH SUBSTANCE ACCORDING TO ITS NATURE, BUT COORDINATED WITH GREAT WISDOM AND PROVIDENCE BY GOD.

IT'S PART OF WHAT MAKES ME THE BEST!

ONE OF LEIBNIZ'S LIFELONG PROJECTS WAS TO USE HIS PHILOSOPHY TO HEAL THE SCHISM BETWEEN CATHOLICS AND PROTESTANTS.

CAN'T WE ALL JUST GET ALONG?

SO HE SENT AN OUTLINE OF THE *DISCOURSE ON METAPHYSICS* TO ANTOINE ARNAULD, A PROMINENT, BUT HIGHLY CONTROVERSIAL, CATHOLIC THEOLOGIAN WHOM HE GOT TO KNOW IN PARIS.

SUCH AN ERUDITE AND REASONABLE PERSON WOULD HAVE TO APPROVE SUCH BEAUTIFUL IDEAS.

ARNAULD WAS A LEADING FIGURE IN FRANCE OF THE JANSENIST MOVEMENT — A SMALL, AUSTERE CATHOLIC SECT.

THE JANSENISTS WERE PERSECUTED BY THE FRENCH CROWN AND THE CHURCH HIERARCHY FOR THEIR VIEWS ON DIVINE GRACE AND OTHER MATTERS.

BUT THEY RESISTED ANY COMPROMISE OF THEIR PRINCIPLES.

ARNAULD WAS A BRILLIANT BUT STUBBORN MAN, AND NOT ONE TO CONCEDE A MILLIMETER TO HIS MANY ENEMIES.

WE WILL NEVER GIVE IN. GOD IS ON OUR SIDE.

HE WAS ALSO A GIFTED PHILOSOPHER. AS A YOUNG SCHOLAR, HE HAD, LIKE HOBBES, SUBMITTED A SET OF OBJECTIONS TO DESCARTES'S *MEDITATIONS.*

THESE ARE THE BEST OF THEM ALL.

AMONG OTHER THINGS, ARNAULD WONDERED HOW DESCARTES COULD USE HIS INTELLECT TO PROVE GOD'S EXISTENCE AND BENEFICENCE AND THEREBY VALIDATE THE RELIABILITY OF HIS INTELLECT.

IT SEEMS TO ME THAT YOU'RE ARGUING IN A CIRCLE!

ARNAULD WAS IN EXILE FROM FRANCE WHEN HE READ LEIBNIZ'S OUTLINE.

WELL, THIS SHOULD BE INTERESTING.

HE WAS NOT IMPRESSED, TO SAY THE LEAST (ALTHOUGH HE ADMITS HE WAS SICK WHEN HE READ IT).

THESE ARE HORRIFYING IDEAS. (COUGH!) NO CATHOLIC COULD POSSIBLY ACCEPT THEM.

MONSIEUR LEIBNIZ, I SUGGEST YOU GIVE UP DOING METAPHYSICS...

"...AND TURN YOUR ATTENTION TO YOUR OWN SALVATION"?

ARNAULD WAS KNOWN TO BE IRASCIBLE, BUT HIS HARSH AND INSULTING RESPONSE TOOK LEIBNIZ BY SURPRISE.

WHAT A HOT-HEAD!

IT'S NO WONDER HE DOESN'T HAVE ANY FRIENDS LEFT.

WHAT ESPECIALLY BOTHERED ARNAULD WERE THE APPARENT CONSEQUENCES OF LEIBNIZ'S VIEWS FOR DIVINE AND HUMAN LIBERTY.

MAYBE GOD WAS FREE TO CREATE OR NOT CREATE THIS WORLD.

BUT ONCE IT WAS CREATED...

...EVERYTHING THAT HAS SINCE HAPPENED TO THE HUMAN RACE OR WILL EVER HAPPEN TO IT OCCURS BY A FATALISTIC NECESSITY.

GOD WILL HAVE NO SAY OVER THE COURSE OF HISTORY...

ONCE GOD HAS CREATED *THIS* WORLD

WITH *THIS* ADAM,

ADAM WILL NECESSARILY EAT THE FRUIT,

AND THERE IS NOTHING GOD CAN DO ABOUT IT OR ANYTHING ELSE.

...NOR WILL HUMAN BEINGS HAVE ANY FREEDOM.

ACCORDING TO YOUR VIEW OF SUBSTANCE, ADAM'S EATING THE FRUIT CANNOT BE A FREE CHOICE!

LEIBNIZ THOUGHT THAT ARNAULD DID NOT REALLY UNDERSTAND HIS VIEWS.

GOD KNEW EVERY LAST DETAIL OF THE WORLD THAT WOULD BE CREATED,

NOTHING HAPPENS INDEPENDENTLY OF GOD'S INTENTIONS.

AND CHOSE THIS PARTICULAR WORLD WITH THIS PARTICULAR ADAM OVER ALL OTHERS,

JUST *BECAUSE* IT INVOLVED THIS COURSE OF EVENTS.

THE PUGNACIOUS ARNAULD WAS NOT PERSUADED.

FORTUNATELY FOR LEIBNIZ, ARNAULD, ON THE RUN FROM THE AUTHORITIES, HAD MORE PRESSING MATTERS TO DEAL WITH.

YOU CAN SAY THAT AGAIN.

ALL THIS NECESSITY SEEMS AWFULLY CLOSE TO WHAT SPINOZA WAS SAYING!

WHOOPS. GOTTA GO!

ACTIVITY AND SPONTANEITY WERE NOT THE ONLY DEFINING FEATURES OF SUBSTANCE FOR LEIBNIZ.

A SUBSTANCE ALSO HAD TO BE A TRUE *UNITY*.

IT HAD TO BE REALLY *ONE* THING AND NOT *SIMPLY* A COLLECTION OF THINGS (LIKE A PILE OF ROCKS)

OR A "MERE PHENOMENON" (LIKE A RAINBOW).

THESE THINGS ARE "ONE" ONLY IN THE MIND OF A PERCEIVER.

BUT NOW THERE IS A PROBLEM.

CAN A BODY BE A SUBSTANCE?

CAN A SUBSTANCE INVOLVE MATTER AT ALL?

THE PROBLEM IS THAT MATTER IS DIVISIBLE INTO EXTENDED PARTS, AND THOSE EXTENDED PARTS DIVISIBLE INTO FURTHER EXTENDED PARTS,

THE DIVISION OF MATTER

NEVER

ENDS.

AND SO ON.

WHAT SEEMED TO BE ONE THING – A MATERIAL BODY – TURNS OUT TO BE ONLY AN INFINITELY DIVISIBLE AGGREGATE, AND NOT REAL AT ALL.

THIS QUESTION PUZZLED LEIBNIZ THROUGHOUT HIS PHILOSOPHICAL CAREER.

At first, Leibniz allowed that there were corporeal substances.

There's a difference between my cat and a pile of rocks.

But a corporeal *substance* has to be more than just passive, divisible extension.

It requires some unifying and animating element,

A living cat is a substance.

Something to make it truly one organic thing.

Its unity and activity come from a soul-like form added to its matter.

A dead cat is just a bunch of matter.

I'll miss you, Meow-chiavelli.

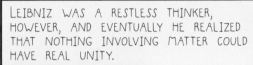
LEIBNIZ WAS A RESTLESS THINKER, HOWEVER, AND EVENTUALLY HE REALIZED THAT NOTHING INVOLVING MATTER COULD HAVE REAL UNITY.

ONLY AN ABSOLUTELY SIMPLE THING, SOMETHING THAT DOES NOT HAVE ANY PARTS WHATSOEVER, IS REALLY "ONE."

AND THE ONLY THINGS THAT ARE ABSOLUTELY SIMPLE AND TRULY INDIVISIBLE ARE SPIRITUAL: MINDS OR SOULS.

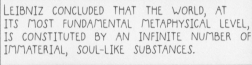
LEIBNIZ CONCLUDED THAT THE WORLD, AT ITS MOST FUNDAMENTAL METAPHYSICAL LEVEL, IS CONSTITUTED BY AN INFINITE NUMBER OF IMMATERIAL, SOUL-LIKE SUBSTANCES.

I CALL THEM "MONADS." THEY ARE SINGULAR SIMPLE UNITIES.

AS SUBSTANCE, A MONAD IS THE ACTIVE SOURCE OF ALL ITS OWN STATES AND ACTIVITIES.

ONE CREATED MONAD CANNOT HAVE A CAUSAL INFLUENCE UPON THE INNER BEING OF ANOTHER MONAD.

MONADS HAVE NO WINDOWS THROUGH WHICH ANYTHING MAY GO IN OR COME OUT.

BECAUSE MONADS ARE IMMATERIAL, THEY DO NOT OCCUPY SPACE. AND BECAUSE MONADS ARE MIND-LIKE, THEIR INNER STATES ARE "PERCEPTIONS," WITH CHANGES IN THE PERCEPTIONS OF EACH MONAD REFLECTING CHANGES IN THE OTHERS.

THE PERCEPTIONS OF ALL THE MONADS IN THE WORLD ARE PERFECTLY COORDINATED THROUGH THE PRE-ESTABLISHED HARMONY.

THIS IS WHY IT *SEEMS* AS IF THERE IS CAUSAL INTER-ACTION

AMONG THINGS IN THE WORLD.

IN LEIBNIZ'S *MONADOLOGY*, EVERY THING IN NATURE IS AGGREGATED OUT OF MONADS.

THESE SPIRITUAL SUBSTANCES ARE WHAT IS REALLY REAL.

WHAT APPEARS AS THE *MATERIAL* WORLD — BODIES IN SPACE — EXISTS ONLY WITHIN THE PERCEPTIONS OF MONADS.

MONADS ARE THE TRUE ATOMS OF NATURE AND THE BASIC ELEMENTS OF ALL THINGS.

LEIBNIZ WAS NOT THE ONLY 17TH-CENTURY THINKER TO ADOPT A SPIRITUAL MONISM –

THE VIEW THAT EVERYTHING IN NATURE IS "FULL OF LIFE AND PERCEPTION."

HE MAY HAVE BEEN INFLUENCED BY WHAT HE READ IN A LATIN TRANSLATION OF A BOOK

BY A LEARNED MEMBER OF THE ENGLISH ARISTOCRACY.

CAMBRIDGE AND LONDON

1650

LADY ANNE CONWAY WAS AN ENGLISH PHILOSOPHER.

BECAUSE WOMEN WERE NOT PERMITTED TO ATTEND UNIVERSITIES, SHE RECEIVED HER PHILOSOPHICAL TUTORING THROUGH CORRESPONDENCE WITH HENRY MORE,

A PHILOSOPHER AT THE UNIVERSITY OF CAMBRIDGE.

MORE WAS BOTH A PROPONENT AND A CRITIC OF DESCARTES'S PHILOSOPHY.

HE BELIEVED THAT THE DUALISM OF MIND AND BODY FURTHERED THE AIMS OF RELIGION.

THERE IS NO BETTER WAY TO PROVE THE IMMORTALITY OF THE SOUL.

I COULDN'T AGREE MORE!

BUT MORE WAS TROUBLED BY DESCARTES'S CLAIM THAT ANIMALS DO NOT HAVE SOULS...

IF ANIMALS DON'T HAVE SOULS,

WHAT'S TO KEEP A MATERIALIST FROM ARGUING THAT WE DON'T EITHER?

...AND MORE GENERALLY BY A MECHANICAL PHILOSOPHY THAT EMPTIED THE WORLD OF ALL SPIRITUAL ELEMENTS, LEAVING BEHIND ONLY INERT, PASSIVE MATTER.

SUCH A VIEW CAUSES SERIOUS PROBLEMS FOR PHYSICS...

WHAT WILL ACCOUNT FOR MOTION?

AND EVEN MORE SERIOUS PROBLEMS FOR RELIGION.

A WORLD WITHOUT SOULS, WITHOUT LIFE: DOES THIS NOT LEAD TO ATHEISM?

MORE BELIEVED THAT THERE HAD TO BE MORE TO NATURE THAN JUST MATTER.

EVERY BODY IS ALIVE WITH THOUGHT. ONLY THIS CAN EXPLAIN ALL THE ACTIVITY WE SEE IN THE WORLD.

MORE'S "SPIRIT OF NATURE" IS AN ACTIVE, IMMATERIAL PRINCIPLE THAT EMANATES FROM GOD.

THIS SPIRITUAL SUBSTANCE IS DISTINCT FROM MATTER ITSELF BUT PRESENT IN ALL MATERIAL BODIES.

IT PLAYS AN IMPORTANT ROLE IN MORE'S PHYSICS OF MOTION...

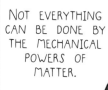

NOT EVERYTHING CAN BE DONE BY THE MECHANICAL POWERS OF MATTER.

AND IN HIS PERENNIAL CAMPAIGN AGAINST MATERIALISM AND ATHEISM.

THE VISCOUNTESS CONWAY LEARNED A GREAT DEAL FROM HER CAMBRIDGE TUTOR AND FRIEND, BUT WENT ONE STEP FURTHER.

IT WAS NOT ENOUGH TO SAY THAT A SPIRITUAL POWER IS ADDED TO THE INERT MATTER OF BODIES.

GOD, AN INFINITE SPIRIT, COULD NOT HAVE CREATED SOMETHING SO UNLIKE HIMSELF AS MERE LIFELESS MATTER.

EVERYTHING CREATED BY GOD MUST BE SIMILAR TO GOD IN SOME RESPECT.

A BODY, THEN, IS NOT A DEAD MASS WITHOUT ANY LIFE OR PERFECTION.

IN *THE PRINCIPLES OF THE MOST ANCIENT AND MODERN PHILOSOPHY,* CONWAY REJECTED EVEN MORE'S BRAND OF DUALISM AND ARGUED THAT THERE IS AN ESSENTIAL SIMILARITY BETWEEN MIND AND MATTER.

SPIRIT AND BODY ARE OF THE SAME NATURE.

EVERY BODY CAN CHANGE INTO A SPIRIT AND EVERY SPIRIT INTO A BODY.

ACCORDING TO CONWAY'S VITALISM, ALL BODIES ARE ESSENTIALLY ALIVE, ACTIVE, AND THINKING.

EVERY BODY IS A CERTAIN LIFE OR SPIRIT WITH A PRINCIPLE OF PERCEPTION.

THE SIMILARITY IN NATURE BETWEEN BODY AND SPIRIT EXPLAINS HOW THE HUMAN MIND AND THE HUMAN BODY CAN BE UNITED AND INTERACT.

MY PHILOSOPHY IMPROVES UPON ANY DUALISM

THAT CLAIMS THAT BODY IS MERELY EXTENSION AND INCAPABLE OF LIFE AND PERCEPTION.

BUT CONWAY WAS NOT AIMING ONLY AT DESCARTES.

IT ALSO REFUTES HOBBES,

WHO HOLDS THAT THERE ARE NO INCORPOREAL SUBSTANCES...

...AS WELL AS SPINOZA,

WHO MAKES GOD AND CREATURES INTO ONE THING.

THERE WAS ANOTHER PHILOSOPHER BESIDES SPINOZA WHO INTRIGUED AND TROUBLED LEIBNIZ AS HE DEVELOPED HIS PHILOSOPHY.

DURING HIS YEARS IN PARIS, LEIBNIZ MET A CATHOLIC PRIEST AND THEOLOGIAN WHOSE DEVOTION TO BOTH DESCARTES AND SAINT AUGUSTINE LED HIM TO SOME VERY STRANGE AND UNORTHODOX IDEAS.

I'M NOT SURE WHETHER THIS GUY IS BRILLIANT...

OR CRAZY.

PARIS

1675

ONE DAY, NICOLAS MALEBRANCHE WAS WALKING ALONG THE RIVER SEINE WHEN HE CAME UPON A COPY OF DESCARTES'S *TREATISE ON MAN* IN A BOOKSTALL.

WELL, WHAT HAVE WE HERE?

MALEBRANCHE BECAME SO EXCITED BY WHAT HE READ THAT HE HAD TO PUT THE BOOK DOWN TO CATCH HIS BREATH.

BE STILL MY BEATING HEART!

HE WENT RIGHT TO WORK BUILDING ON DESCARTES'S IDEAS.

I CAN MAKE IT BETTER!

BIGGER!

STRONGER!

HOWEVER, MALEBRANCHE WAS NO ORDINARY CARTESIAN,

A LITTLE BIT OF DESCARTES,

AND HE WENT WELL BEYOND ANYTHING THAT DESCARTES HIMSELF WOULD HAVE SANCTIONED.

A LITTLE BIT OF *SAINT AUGUSTINE*...

MALEBRANCHE WAS ALSO, AT ONE TIME, FRIENDS WITH ANTOINE ARNAULD.

THAT IS, UNTIL ARNAULD STARTED READING MALEBRANCHE'S *THE SEARCH AFTER TRUTH.*

WHAT?

AND *TREATISE ON NATURE AND GRACE.*

WHAT??

MALEBRANCHE GOT A GOOD TASTE OF THE CANTANKEROUS JANSENIST'S TEMPER.

WHY DIDN'T YOU FIRST ASK ME FOR ADVICE BEFORE PUBLISHING SUCH RISKY FOLLY?

I DID, BUT YOU NEVER RESPONDED, MONSIEUR "OH, I'M EVER SO BUSY"!

MALEBRANCHE ENTHUSIASTICALLY ADOPTED DESCARTES'S METAPHYSICS.

MIND IS THINKING SUBSTANCE,

BODY IS EXTENDED SUBSTANCE,

AND THEY HAVE NOTHING IN COMMON.

BUT HE, LIKE OTHER PHILOSOPHERS, REALIZED THAT THIS STRICT DUALISM GAVE RISE TO SERIOUS PROBLEMS IN PHYSICS.

IF A BODY IS JUST EXTENSION, THEN IT IS PASSIVE AND INERT.

IT HAS NO FORCE, NO ACTIVE CAUSAL POWER TO MOVE ITSELF OR ANY OTHER BODY.

STOP THAT!

HOW, THEN, DO BODIES MOVE AT ALL?

AND WHY DO THEY MOVE THE WAY THEY DO?

IN FACT, MALEBRANCHE CLAIMED THAT *NO* SUBSTANCE IN NATURE HAS ANY TRUE CAUSAL POWERS. BODIES DO NOT CAUSE EFFECTS IN OTHER BODIES OR IN MINDS.

AND MINDS DO NOT CAUSE EFFECTS IN BODIES OR EVEN IN THEMSELVES.

POWER BELONGS TO GOD ALONE.

AND... ACTION!

GOD IS THE SOLE, DIRECT, AND IMMEDIATE CAUSE OF EVERY EVENT IN NATURE.

MALEBRANCHE DEFENDED THIS RADICAL THESIS WITH A VARIETY OF METAPHYSICAL ARGUMENTS.

IT'S NOT SO ORIGINAL - IT'S ALL THERE IN DESCARTES.

OK, WELL, MAYBE NOT ALL OF IT.

According to the doctrine of divine conservation, God does not just create a world that then has an independent existence of its own.

After creating the world, God must conserve it and every particular thing in it in existence from moment to moment.

It's as if the original act of creation never ends.

When conserving a body, God must at each moment put that body in some place relative to other bodies.

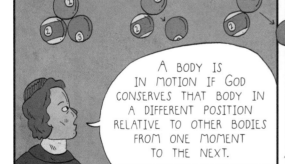

A body is in motion if God conserves that body in a different position relative to other bodies from one moment to the next.

And a body is at rest if God conserves it in the same relative place.

SO BODIES MOVE ONLY BECAUSE GOD MOVES THEM.

THE IMPACT OF ONE BODY UPON ANOTHER IS NOT THE *CAUSE* OF THE MOTION OF THE SECOND BODY...

BUT SIMPLY AN *OCCASION* FOR GOD TO MOVE THAT BODY, ACCORDING TO THE LAWS OF NATURE.

BUT THEN NEITHER CAN A HUMAN MIND MOVE A BODY.

A VOLITION IN THE MIND IS JUST AN OCCASION FOR GOD TO MOVE SOME PART OF THAT BODY, ACCORDING TO THE LAWS OF MIND-BODY UNION.

NO MORE PROBLEMS ABOUT HOW MINDS AND BODIES CAN INTERACT.

THEY DON'T!

MALEBRANCHE ALSO ARGUES FOR HIS "OCCASIONALISM" FROM AN ANALYSIS OF THE NATURE OF CAUSATION.

THERE IS A *NECESSARY CONNECTION* BETWEEN A CAUSE AND ITS EFFECT.

IF THE CAUSE HAPPENS, THE EFFECT *MUST* HAPPEN.

BUT THERE IS *NO* NECESSARY CONNECTION BETWEEN WHAT I WILL

AND WHAT MY BODY DOES.

BECAUSE HUMAN BEINGS ARE NOT OMNIPOTENT, IT IS CONCEIVABLE THAT A PERSON WILLS TO RAISE HER ARM BUT HER ARM DOES NOT RISE.

COME ON...

NO NECESSITY THERE!

BUT IF *GOD* WILLS THAT SOMETHING SHOULD HAPPEN, IT *NECESSARILY* HAPPENS.

GOD'S + WILL

THAT IS JUST WHAT IT MEANS TO BE OMNIPOTENT.

THUS, THERE IS AN ABSOLUTELY NECESSARY CONNECTION ONLY BETWEEN THE WILL OF GOD AND SOME EVENT.

SO GOD IS THE TRUE CAUSE OF EVERYTHING THAT HAPPENS IN BODIES.

AND IN MINDS.

GOD CAUSES A BODY AT REST TO BEGIN TO MOVE WHEN IT IS STRUCK BY ANOTHER BODY.

AND GOD CAUSES A BODY TO MOVE WHEN A MIND WILLS THAT IT SHOULD MOVE.

GOD ALSO CAUSES SENSATIONS IN THE MIND WHEN THE BODY IS AFFECTED IN A CERTAIN WAY.

WHEN I AM IMPALED BY A SHARP OBJECT, GOD CAUSES ME TO FEEL PAIN.

AND WHEN I WILL TO REMOVE THE SHARP OBJECT FROM MY BODY, GOD MOVES MY MUSCLES SO THAT THE ARM MOVES TOWARD THE PAINFUL SPOT.

BODILY MOTIONS AND MENTAL STATES ARE NOTHING MORE THAN OCCASIONS FOR GOD TO ACT.

THE IDEA THAT THINGS IN THE WORLD AROUND US ARE TRUE CAUSES LEADS TO HEATHEN IDOLATRY - WE WOULD WORSHIP THEM, RATHER THAN GOD, AS CAPABLE OF MAKING US HAPPY.

KIND OF CRAZY, ISN'T IT?

NATURE IS NOW FULL OF MIRACLES, SINCE EVERYTHING IS BROUGHT ABOUT BY GOD.

YOU DON'T UNDERSTAND WHAT A MIRACLE IS. JUST BECAUSE SOMETHING IS CAUSED BY GOD DOESN'T MAKE IT A MIRACLE.

A MIRACLE IS SOMETHING THAT HAPPENS THAT SURPASSES THE POWERS OF NATURAL SUBSTANCES. ON YOUR VIEW, EVERYTHING IS A MIRACLE, SINCE NATURAL SUBSTANCES HAVE NO POWERS AT ALL.

AS IF! A MIRACLE IS AN EVENT THAT IS A VIOLATION OF THE LAWS OF NATURE. AND GOD'S CAUSAL ACTIVITY IN THE WORLD REGULARLY FOLLOWS THE LAWS OF NATURE.

WELL, AT LEAST WE AGREE THAT FINITE SUBSTANCES DO NOT INTERACT.

ALWAYS THE OPTIMIST, GOTTFRIED!

MALEBRANCHE WAS, LIKE LEIBNIZ, MOVED BY THE PROBLEM OF EVIL.

WHY DO VIRTUOUS PEOPLE SOMETIMES SUFFER AND WICKED PEOPLE PROSPER IN A WORLD CREATED BY A WISE AND JUST GOD?

YOU HAVE TO UNDERSTAND THAT GOD MUST ACT IN THE MOST WORTHY WAY.

AND SO GOD ALWAYS ACTS IN A SIMPLE, GENERAL, AND UNIFORM MANNER — NEVER THROUGH PARTICULAR AND *AD HOC* VOLITIONS.

WHAT THIS MEANS IS THAT GOD CHOSE, AMONG ALL POSSIBLE WORLDS, THE ONE THAT WAS GOVERNED BY THE SIMPLEST LAWS.

AND GOD'S REGULAR CAUSAL ACTIVITY SIMPLY CARRIES OUT THOSE LAWS.

UNFORTUNATELY, SIMPLE AND GENERAL LAWS DO NOT TAKE ACCOUNT OF EVERYONE'S PARTICULAR NEEDS AND EXPECTATIONS.

The laws of nature do not always have the best consequences for every individual.

Sometimes it will rain on my parade.

God could intervene and, by a particular and *ad hoc* volition, stop the rain from falling...

Or prevent a tsunami from destroying a coastal village...

Or keep a virtuous person from suffering at the hands of a wicked person.

But that would require God to act contrary to the laws of nature.

And we should not expect constant miracles from God.

GOD WILL NOT DEPART FROM THE MOST WORTHY, SIMPLE, AND GENERAL WAYS JUST FOR THE CONVENIENCE OF INDIVIDUAL CREATURES.

GOD WOULD PREFER THAT THE EVILS DID NOT EXIST, BUT STILL ALLOWS THEM TO HAPPEN.

LEIBNIZ WAS IMPRESSED, BUT ARNAULD WAS SCANDALIZED. SHOCKED. APOPLECTIC!

WHAT? GOD HAS PREFERENCES THAT CANNOT BE CARRIED OUT? VOLITIONS THAT ARE INEFFECTIVE?

SO MUCH FOR GOD'S OMNIPOTENCE! WHAT A PATHETIC DEITY, WHO CAN'T DO WHAT HE WANTS.

WELL, *YOU* CAN HAVE GOD'S ARBITRARY POWER, BUT I'D RATHER HAVE A GOD OF WISDOM AND JUSTICE.

GOD IS GUIDED BY WHAT IS RIGHT.

WELL, YOU DON'T KNOW YOUR DESCARTES *OR* YOUR AUGUSTINE!

AND *YOU*, SIR, ARE NOTHING BUT A PROTESTANT IN DISGUISE!

GUYS! CAN'T WE JUST ENJOY BRUNCH?

ARNAULD AND MALEBRANCHE WOULD FIGHT IT OUT WITH MUCH PASSION FOR THE NEXT TEN YEARS.

THEIR DEBATE WAS ONE OF THE GREAT INTELLECTUAL EVENTS OF THE 17TH CENTURY.

IT SEEMS TO ME THAT MR. ARNAULD HAS TOO HOT A TEMPER, AND THAT MR. MALEBRANCHE IS A LITTLE OUT OF HIS MIND.

LONDON

1689

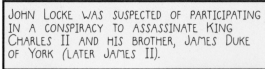

IN 1683, AN OXFORD-TRAINED ENGLISH PHILOSOPHER LEFT HIS HOMELAND IN A HURRY.

CHEERIO!

JOHN LOCKE WAS SUSPECTED OF PARTICIPATING IN A CONSPIRACY TO ASSASSINATE KING CHARLES II AND HIS BROTHER, JAMES DUKE OF YORK (LATER JAMES II).

THIS IS THE GUY WE'RE LOOKING FOR.

WHILE HE WAS NO FRIEND OF THE STUART MONARCHY, LOCKE WAS PROBABLY NOT A PART OF THE CONSPIRACY.

STILL, BETTER SAFE THAN SORRY.

I'D BETTER GET OUT OF HERE BEFORE THEY COME FOR ME.

ALONG WITH HIS PATRON AND FRIEND THE EARL OF SHAFTESBURY, LOCKE TOOK OFF FOR THE NETHERLANDS.

HE WOULD NOT RETURN TO ENGLAND UNTIL SIX YEARS LATER, JUST BEHIND WILLIAM OF ORANGE AND HIS CONQUERING ARMY.

Once settled in Amsterdam, and concerned for England's future after the Catholic James II took the throne, Locke put quill to paper to add the finishing touches on his *Treatises on Government.*

In these essays, Locke explains the theoretical origin and true purpose of civil society.

It's time to put the "divine right of kings" to rest for good.

SMACK!

Locke, like Hobbes, sees the basis of society in an agreement that emerges from a state of nature.

BUT LOCKE'S ORIGINAL CONDITION IS A MORE BENIGN PLACE THAN WHAT HIS OLDER ENGLISH COLLEAGUE CONCEIVED.

THE STATE OF NATURE IS NOT A STATE OF WAR.

IT'S JUST PEOPLE LIVING ACCORDING TO REASON WITHOUT A COMMON AND SUPERIOR AUTHORITY TO JUDGE BETWEEN THEM.

IT IS A CONDITION OF PERFECT FREEDOM AND EQUALITY, WHERE EVERYONE MAY ORDER THEIR LIVES AS THEY SEE FIT.

THEY DO NOT, HOWEVER, HAVE ABSOLUTE LICENSE TO DO WHATEVER THEY WANT.

HEY!

EVEN IN THE STATE OF NATURE, WHERE THERE IS NO SOVEREIGN, LORD, OR MASTER,

SCREEEEEECH!

...THERE ARE STILL LAWS.

CERTAIN MORAL PRINCIPLES ARE VALID FOR ALL HUMAN BEINGS NO MATTER WHO THEY ARE OR WHEN OR WHERE THEY LIVE.

THE LAW OF NATURE IS INDEPENDENT OF DIVINE DECREES AND CIVIL LEGISLATION.

NATURAL LAW IS DISCOVERABLE BY REASON ALONE AND GOVERNS LIFE IN THE STATE OF NATURE.

IT PROCLAIMS THAT EACH PERSON MUST STRIVE TO PRESERVE HIMSELF, AND TO PRESERVE OTHERS AS MUCH AS HE CAN.

NO ONE MAY HARM ANOTHER IN HIS LIFE, LIBERTY, HEALTH, OR POSSESSIONS.

IN THE ABSENCE OF GOVERNMENT,

ANYONE HAS THE RIGHT TO ENFORCE THE LAW OF NATURE

AND PUNISH THOSE WHO TRANSGRESS IT.

IN THIS ANARCHIC BUT GENERALLY PEACEFUL CONDITION, A PERSON ACQUIRES PROPERTY BY "MIXING HIS LABOR" WITH SOMETHING.

HE ALSO ACQUIRES A *RIGHT* TO WHATEVER HE THEREBY MAKES HIS OWN —

LAND HE HAS CULTIVATED,

A TABLE HE HAS BUILT,

OR AN APPLE HE HAS BAKED INTO A PIE.

UNFORTUNATELY, THE STATE OF NATURE IS NOT ALWAYS SO PEACEFUL. INEQUALITIES WILL ARISE...

...AND THERE WILL INEVITABLY BE DISPUTES OVER PROPERTY.

HEY! THAT'S MINE!

AN INCONVENIENCE OF THE STATE OF NATURE AND A THREAT TO ITS PEACE IS THAT, IN THE ABSENCE OF AN ACKNOWLEDGED CENTRAL AUTHORITY, EVERY PERSON IS THE JUDGE

OF HIS OWN CASE.

INDIVIDUALS GUIDED BY REASON WILL THUS SEEK TO LEAVE THE STATE OF NATURE BY FORMING A CIVIL SOCIETY THAT CAN PROTECT THEIR NATURAL RIGHTS TO LIFE, LIBERTY, AND PROPERTY.

THE PURPOSE OF THE STATE IS NOT TO ABOLISH OR RESTRAIN FREEDOM, BUT TO PRESERVE AND ENLARGE IT.

A COMMONWEALTH IS CREATED WHEN EACH PERSON VOLUNTARILY GIVES UP HIS NATURAL POWER TO ENFORCE HIS RIGHTS AND HANDS IT OVER TO THE COMMUNITY-AT-LARGE.

POWER

WHEREVER A NUMBER OF PEOPLE UNITE INTO ONE SOCIETY SO AS TO QUIT EVERY ONE HIS EXECUTIVE POWER OF THE LAW OF NATURE AND RESIGN IT TO THE PUBLIC, THERE AND THERE ONLY IS POLITICAL OR CIVIL SOCIETY.

ONLY THROUGH CONSENT OF THE GOVERNED - AND NEVER THROUGH FORCE OR DIVINE DECREE -

IS THERE LEGITIMATE GOVERNMENT, AUTHORIZED TO MAKE AND ENFORCE LAWS FOR THE PUBLIC GOOD.

THROUGH THIS ORIGINAL COMPACT, EVERY PERSON OBLIGES HIMSELF TO SUBMIT TO THE DETERMINATION OF THE MAJORITY.

FOR LOCKE, ABSOLUTE MONARCHY, WITH NO SEPARATION OF EXECUTIVE, JUDICIAL, AND LEGISLATIVE POWERS, IS INCONSISTENT WITH CIVIL SOCIETY.

THERE WOULD BE NO AUTHORITY ABOVE THE ABSOLUTE MONARCH TO APPEAL TO FOR RESOLVING DIFFERENCES WITH SUCH A RULER AND TO SEEK REDRESS AGAINST HIM.

IN THIS, LOCKE DIFFERS FROM HOBBES.

AN ABSOLUTE MONARCH LIVES IN A STATE OF NATURE WITH HIS SUBJECTS.

HE ALSO DEPARTS FROM HOBBES IN ALLOWING FOR REBELLION AGAINST A SOVEREIGN.

SOMETIMES IT'S THE ONLY RECOURSE YOU HAVE.

WHEN A GOVERNMENT FAILS TO UPHOLD ITS END OF THE BARGAIN AND PROTECT LIFE, LIBERTY, AND PROPERTY, THE CITIZENS MAY SEEK TO REPLACE IT.

WHEN A KING BECOMES A TYRANT, THE PEOPLE HAVE THE RIGHT TO RESIST.

LOCKE HOPED THIS LESSON WOULD BE TAKEN TO HEART IN ENGLAND.

LOCKE'S YEARS IN AMSTERDAM WERE NOT WHOLLY OCCUPIED BY POLITICAL THEORY.

EXILE SURE FREES UP A LOT OF TIME.

HE ALSO COMPLETED *AN ESSAY CONCERNING HUMAN UNDERSTANDING*, A STUDY OF THE SOURCES AND NATURE OF HUMAN KNOWLEDGE.

I CAN DO BETTER THAN DESCARTES.

LOCKE DEFENDS A STRICT EMPIRICISM.

ALL OF THE MIND'S IDEAS, ALL THE THOUGHTS IT EVER HAS, COME EITHER DIRECTLY OR INDIRECTLY FROM EXPERIENCE.

SOME EARLY MODERN THINKERS INSISTED THAT THERE ARE IDEAS INNATE IN THE HUMAN INTELLECT — CONCEPTS THAT THE MIND HAS PRIOR TO AND INDEPENDENT OF EXPERIENCE.

GOD PLACED CERTAIN IDEAS IN MY SOUL WHEN CREATING ME.

INBORN IN EVERY MIND ARE CERTAIN "COMMON NOTIONS" OF RELIGION AND MORALITY.

LORD HERBERT OF CHERBURY

THERE ARE TRUTHS THAT EVERY HUMAN BEING INSTINCTIVELY KNOWS.

THERE IS A GOD. GOD IS TO BE WORSHIPPED.

VIRTUE IS ESSENTIAL TO PIETY.

HUNGRY

WICKEDNESS IS TO BE SHUNNED.

AND THERE IS REWARD

AND PUNISHMENT AFTER THIS LIFE.

THESE INNATE IDEAS OR COMMON NOTIONS ARE SUPPOSED TO EXPLAIN HOW WE KNOW CERTAIN TRUTHS *A PRIORI*...

IT'S HOW I KNOW WHAT GOD IS,

WHAT EXTENSION IS,

AND WHAT THE SOUL IS...

AND TO HELP ORGANIZE EXPERIENCE ITSELF.

THESE NOTIONS INFORM AND MOLD OUR AWARENESS OF THINGS IN THE WORLD.

YEAH, RIGHT.

LOCKE DEVOTED THE ENTIRE FIRST BOOK OF THE *ESSAY* TO REFUTING THE DOCTRINE OF INNATE IDEAS.

WHEN I GET THROUGH WITH THEM, THEY'LL WISH THEY NEVER HEARD OF INNATE IDEAS.

THE PROPONENTS OF INNATENESS ALLEGED THAT THERE ARE TRUTHS TO WHICH EVERYONE NATURALLY ASSENTS.

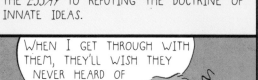

A TRIANGLE HAS THREE SIDES.

GOD IS OUR MAKER AND WE SHOULD WORSHIP HIM.

AND THEY REGARDED INNATE IDEAS, PRESENT IN EVERY MIND, AS THE BEST EXPLANATION OF THIS UNIVERSAL AGREEMENT.

ALRIGHT, GREAT JOB EVERYONE. THAT'S LUNCH.

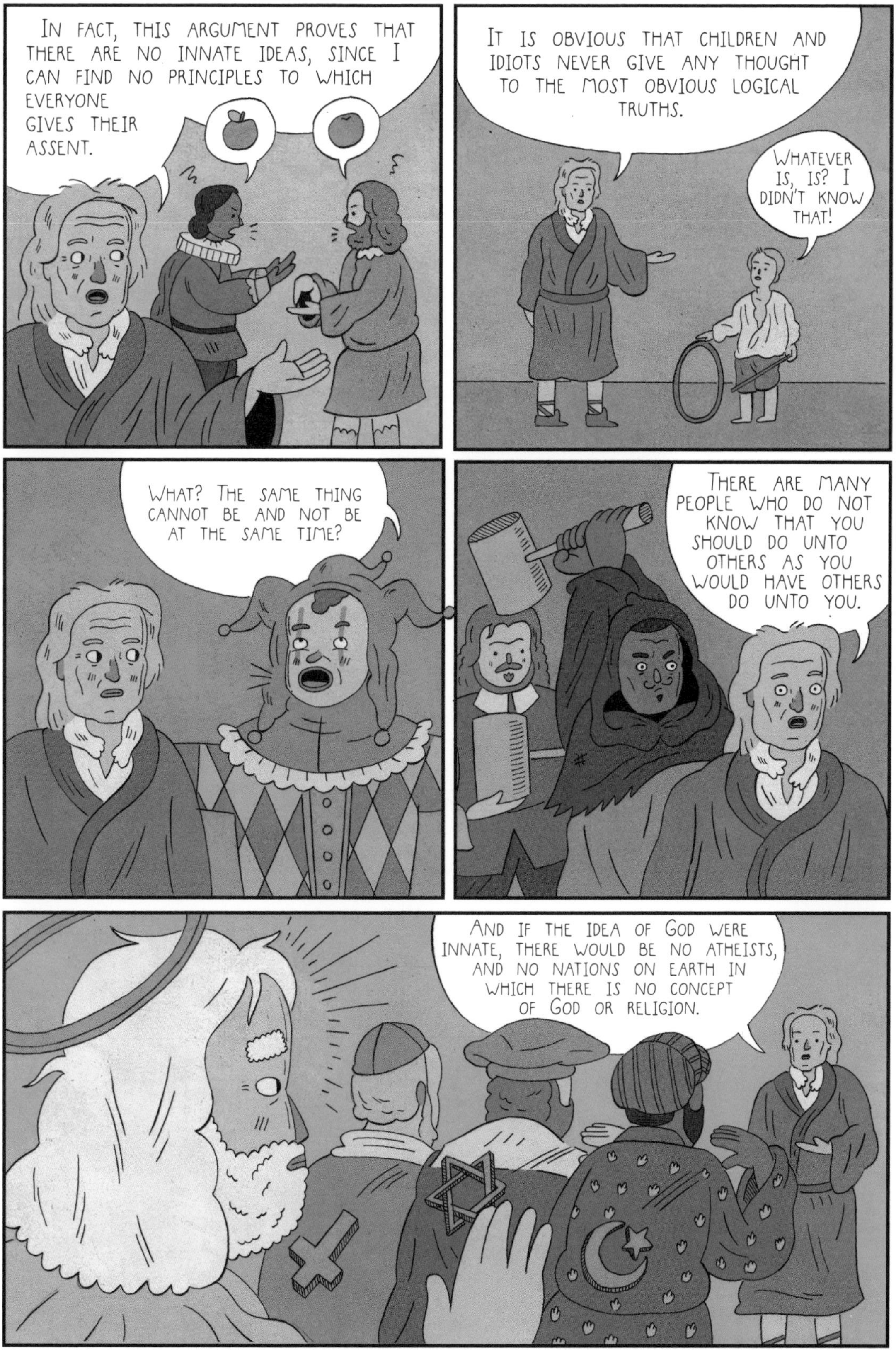
IN FACT, THIS ARGUMENT PROVES THAT THERE ARE NO INNATE IDEAS, SINCE I CAN FIND NO PRINCIPLES TO WHICH EVERYONE GIVES THEIR ASSENT.
IT IS OBVIOUS THAT CHILDREN AND IDIOTS NEVER GIVE ANY THOUGHT TO THE MOST OBVIOUS LOGICAL TRUTHS.
WHATEVER IS, IS? I DIDN'T KNOW THAT!
WHAT? THE SAME THING CANNOT BE AND NOT BE AT THE SAME TIME?
THERE ARE MANY PEOPLE WHO DO NOT KNOW THAT YOU SHOULD DO UNTO OTHERS AS YOU WOULD HAVE OTHERS DO UNTO YOU.
AND IF THE IDEA OF GOD WERE INNATE, THERE WOULD BE NO ATHEISTS, AND NO NATIONS ON EARTH IN WHICH THERE IS NO CONCEPT OF GOD OR RELIGION.

LOCKE CONSIDERS THE REPLY THAT THE INBORN IDEAS AND THE PRINCIPLES THEY GENERATE NEED NOT BE ACTUALLY THOUGHT OR CONSCIOUSLY KNOWN.

WHAT? AN UNCONSCIOUS?

BUT LOCKE REJECTS THIS CLAIM AS ABSURD.

YOU'RE RIGHT! IT'S A RIDICULOUS IDEA.

THERE CAN BE NO TRUTHS IN THE SOUL THAT IT DOES NOT ACTUALLY PERCEIVE OR UNDERSTAND.

NO PROPOSITION CAN BE SAID TO BE IN THE MIND WHICH IT NEVER YET KNEW, WHICH IT WAS NEVER CONSCIOUS OF.

LOCKE INSISTS THAT, IN FACT, THERE IS NO REASON TO POSIT ANY INNATE IDEAS TO EXPLAIN HOW WE KNOW WHAT WE KNOW.

I CAN SHOW HOW WE COME TO ALL THE KNOWLEDGE WE HAVE THROUGH EXPERIENCE AND THE USE OF OUR NATURAL FACULTIES ALONE...

THIS IS THE PROJECT OF THE REST OF THE *ESSAY*.

...WITHOUT ANY NEED FOR INNATE NOTIONS OR PRINCIPLES.

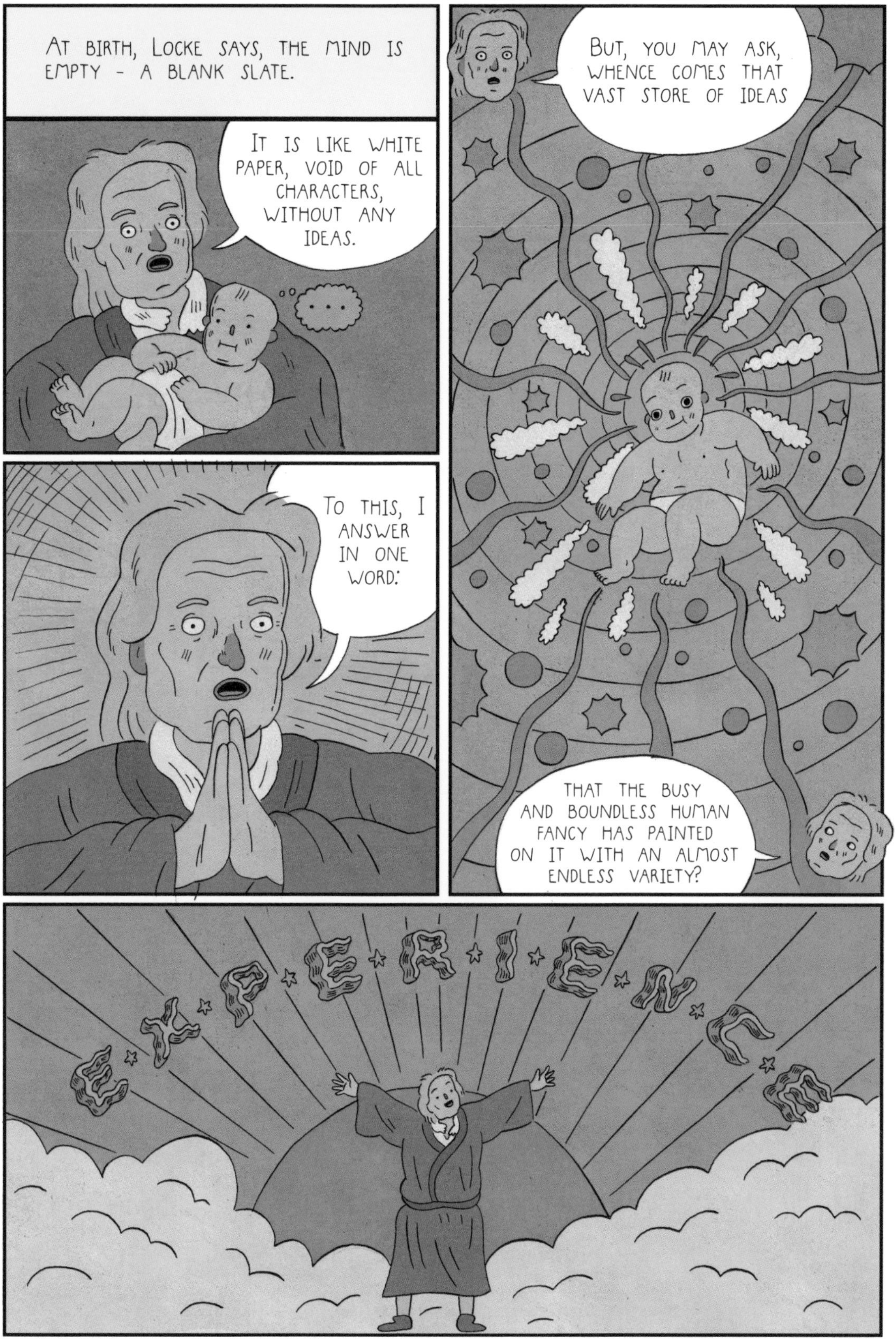

AT BIRTH, LOCKE SAYS, THE MIND IS EMPTY - A BLANK SLATE.
IT IS LIKE WHITE PAPER, VOID OF ALL CHARACTERS, WITHOUT ANY IDEAS.
...
BUT, YOU MAY ASK, WHENCE COMES THAT VAST STORE OF IDEAS
THAT THE BUSY AND BOUNDLESS HUMAN FANCY HAS PAINTED ON IT WITH AN ALMOST ENDLESS VARIETY?
TO THIS, I ANSWER IN ONE WORD:
EXPERIENCE

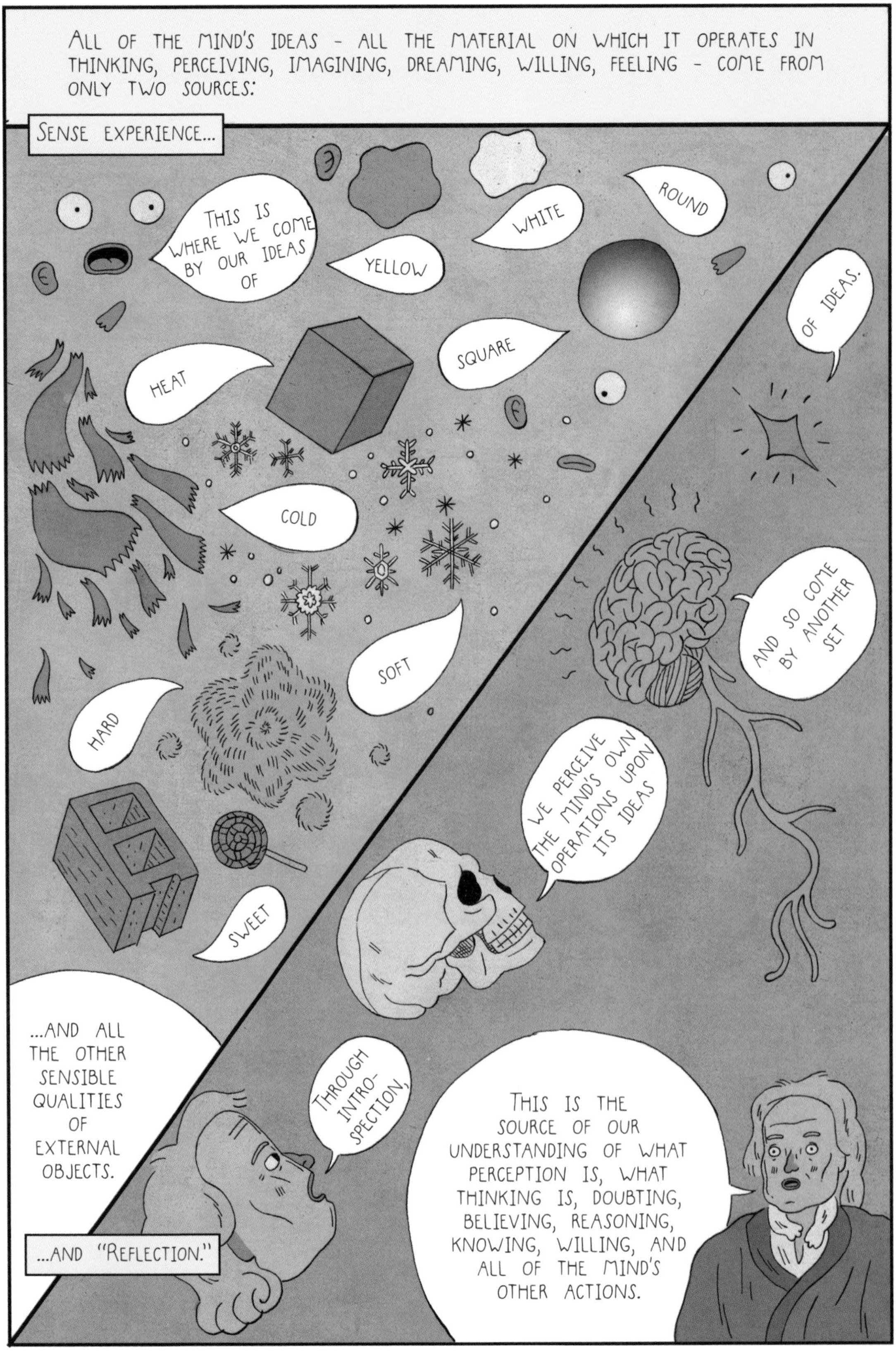
ALL OF THE MIND'S IDEAS - ALL THE MATERIAL ON WHICH IT OPERATES IN THINKING, PERCEIVING, IMAGINING, DREAMING, WILLING, FEELING - COME FROM ONLY TWO SOURCES:
SENSE EXPERIENCE...
THIS IS WHERE WE COME BY OUR IDEAS OF
YELLOW
WHITE
ROUND
HEAT
SQUARE
COLD
SOFT
HARD
SWEET
...AND ALL THE OTHER SENSIBLE QUALITIES OF EXTERNAL OBJECTS.
...AND "REFLECTION."
THROUGH INTRO-SPECTION,
WE PERCEIVE THE MIND'S OWN OPERATIONS UPON ITS IDEAS
AND SO COME BY ANOTHER SET
OF IDEAS.
THIS IS THE SOURCE OF OUR UNDERSTANDING OF WHAT PERCEPTION IS, WHAT THINKING IS, DOUBTING, BELIEVING, REASONING, KNOWING, WILLING, AND ALL OF THE MIND'S OTHER ACTIONS.

SOME OF THE MIND'S IDEAS ARE SIMPLE, SOME ARE COMPLEX.

MY COMPLEX IDEA OF A ROSE IS COMPOSED OF A NUMBER OF SIMPLE IDEAS OF SINGULAR QUALITIES:

THE RED COLOR,

THE FLOWER'S SHAPE,

ITS SWEET SMELL.

SOME OF THE MIND'S COMPLEX IDEAS ARE PASSIVELY RECEIVED BY THE MIND...

SNIFFFFFF

WHILE OTHERS ARE COMPOSED BY THE MIND ITSELF AS IT PUTS TOGETHER A NUMBER OF SIMPLE OR COMPLEX IDEAS.

LOCKE INSISTS THAT THERE ARE NO IDEAS UNACCOUNTED FOR BY HIS THEORY.

EVEN OUR MOST COMPLEX IDEAS ULTIMATELY DERIVE, DIRECTLY OR THROUGH THE MIND'S OWN WORK,

FROM EXPERIENCE.

OH YEAH? WHAT ABOUT THE IDEA OF THE SOUL, AN IMMATERIAL SPIRIT?

EASY. IT'S JUST THE COMBINATION OF THE SIMPLE IDEAS OF THINK-ING...

...AND OF ACTION,

ACQUIRED THROUGH REFLECTION, *WITHOUT* THE IDEAS OF EXTENSION AND SOLIDITY.

HMM. WELL, WHAT ABOUT THE IDEA OF GOD?

NO PROBLEM.

LOCKE WARNS US THAT NOT ALL OF THE SENSORY IDEAS IN THE MIND RESEMBLE THE QUALITIES IN THE EXTERNAL WORLD THAT CAUSE THEM.

THE NATURAL PHILOSOPHER ROBERT BOYLE SET UP HIS LABORATORY IN OXFORD IN 1655.

A FEW YEARS LATER, LOCKE, PURSUING HIS MEDICAL STUDIES, WAS ASSISTING BOYLE WITH EXPERIMENTS IN CHEMISTRY AND OTHER AREAS.

BOYLE WAS THE LEADING ENGLISH PROPONENT OF THE MECHANICAL PHILOSOPHY AND CRITIC OF ARISTOTELIAN FORMS AND QUALITIES.

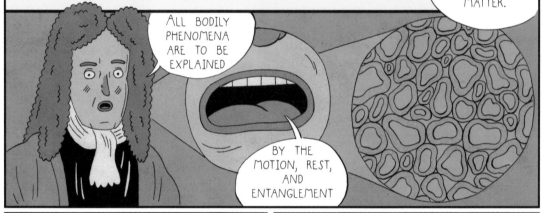

ALL BODILY PHENOMENA ARE TO BE EXPLAINED

BY THE MOTION, REST, AND ENTANGLEMENT

OF "CORPUSCLES," INSENSIBLE PARTICLES OF MATTER.

ANY SINGLE CORPUSCLE HAS ONLY THREE BASIC PROPERTIES: SIZE, SHAPE, AND MOTION OR REST.

THESE, AND THESE ALONE, ARE THE PRIMARY AFFECTIONS OF ANY MATTER.

THE CONGLOMERATION AND ARRANGEMENT OF CORPUSCLES IN A LARGER BODY CONSTITUTES THE "TEXTURE" OF THAT BODY.

WHEN ONE BODY WORKS UPON ANOTHER, THERE IS NOTHING PRODUCED BY THE AGENT IN THE PATIENT EXCEPT SOME LOCAL MOTION IN ITS PARTS OR SOME CHANGE OF TEXTURE CONSEQUENT UPON THAT MOTION.

ALL THE ACTIONS OR POWERS OF ANY BODY, NO MATTER HOW COMPLEX, ARE A FUNCTION SOLELY OF ITS PRIMARY QUALITIES AND ITS TEXTURE.

JUST AS THE CAPACITY OF A KEY TO OPEN A LOCK IS NOT SOME SPIRITUAL OR OCCULT QUALITY IN THE KEY,

BUT ONLY A CONGRUITY BETWEEN THE SHAPE OF THE LOCK AND THE FIGURE OF THE KEY.

LIKEWISE, THE SENSIBLE QUALITIES THAT WE APPREHEND IN BODIES ARE ONLY PERCEPTIONS IN THE MIND

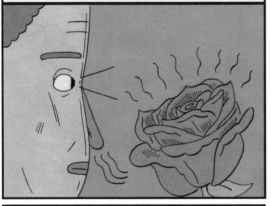

THAT ARE CAUSED BY THE WAY THE CORPUSCULAR TEXTURE OF AN EXTERNAL BODY AFFECTS THE TEXTURE OF THE EYE, THE EAR, AND OTHER SENSES.

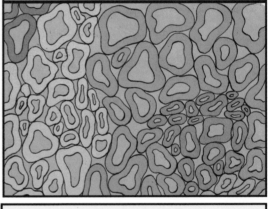

BOYLE HAS A NEW TERM FOR THOSE FEATURES OF BODIES THAT ARE EXPLAINED BY AND REDUCIBLE TO THEIR PRIMARY QUALITIES.

SECONDARY QUALITIES, SUCH AS COLORS AND ODORS,

DEPEND ON THE SIMPLER, MORE PRIMITIVE AFFECTIONS OF MATTER.

BOYLE'S CORPUSCLES ARE DIVISIBLE IN PRINCIPLE (SINCE THEY ARE EXTENDED), AND MAY BE DIVIDED BY GOD.

BUT THEY ARE SO SMALL AND SOLID THAT IN NATURE THEY ARE SCARCELY EVER DIVIDED.

ANOTHER CORPUSCULARIAN WHO INFLUENCED LOCKE WAS THE FRENCH THINKER PIERRE GASSENDI.

GASSENDI TOOK HIS LEAD FROM THE ANCIENT ATOMISM OF EPICURUS.

THE ULTIMATE CONSTITUENTS OF ALL THINGS ARE MINUTE, SOLID, IMPENETRABLE, AND NATURALLY INDIVISIBLE BODIES.

WHAT HE SAID!

GASSENDI'S ATOMS, HOWEVER, WERE NOT LIKE THE INERT MATTER OF MOST MECHANICAL PHILOSOPHIES.

THEY HAVE WEIGHT —

AN INNATE, NATURAL, NATIVE PROPENSITY TO MOTION THAT CANNOT BE LOST, A KIND OF PROPULSION OR IMPETUS FROM WITHIN.

JUST AS EPICUREAN *MINIMA* ARE SURROUNDED BY A VOID, SO GASSENDI'S ATOMS MOVE THROUGH EMPTY SPACE.

THIS ALLOWS ATOMS TO MOVE AWAY FROM AND TOWARD EACH OTHER, BOUNCING OFF OTHER ATOMS

BUT ALSO GETTING TANGLED UP WITH THEM AND FORMING LARGER STRUCTURES.

GASSENDI DID NOT PROCLAIM ATOMISM AS THE ABSOLUTELY CERTAIN AND CONFIRMED TRUTH.

OK, I CONFESS - I'VE NEVER ACTUALLY SEEN AN ATOM.

HE FAVORED A CAUTIOUS, SOMEWHAT SKEPTICAL ATTITUDE IN SCIENCE.

HMPH!

BUT HE WAS DRAWN BY ATOMISM'S FINE HISTORICAL PEDIGREE.

HE ALSO REGARDED IT AS THE BEST EMPIRICAL HYPOTHESIS FOR EXPLAINING THE PHENOMENA.

IT'S WHERE THE EVIDENCE OF SENSE EXPERIENCE LEADS.

IS THERE A BETTER AND SIMPLER WAY TO UNDERSTAND THE SOLIDITY, SHAPE, AND ALL OTHER PROPERTIES AND POWERS OF BODIES THAT WE *DO* SEE...

THAN IN TERMS OF THE SOLIDITY, SHAPE, AND MOTION OF SMALLER BODIES THAT WE DON'T SEE?

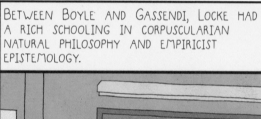

GASSENDI'S EMPIRICISM INCLUDED THE REJECTION OF INNATE IDEAS.

EVERY IDEA IN THE MIND EITHER COMES THROUGH THE SENSES

OR IS FORMED FROM THOSE THAT COME THROUGH THE SENSES.

BETWEEN BOYLE AND GASSENDI, LOCKE HAD A RICH SCHOOLING IN CORPUSCULARIAN NATURAL PHILOSOPHY AND EMPIRICIST EPISTEMOLOGY.

LOCKE, TUTORED BY BOYLE, SAYS THAT SOME IDEAS IN THE MIND RESEMBLE THE *PRIMARY QUALITIES* OF BODIES — THOSE FEATURES THAT BODIES HAVE INDEPENDENTLY OF BEING PERCEIVED.

THE PARTICULAR SIZE, NUMBER, FIGURE, AND MOTION OF THE PARTS OF FIRE OR SNOW ARE REALLY IN THEM,

WHETHER OR NOT ANYONE'S SENSES PERCEIVE THEM.

MY PERCEPTION OF THE *SHAPE* OF A SNOWBALL REPRESENTS A REAL PROPERTY OF THE SNOWBALL.

OTHER SENSORY IDEAS ARE NOT AT ALL LIKE THE FEATURES IN BODIES THAT CAUSE THEM.

THE WHITENESS AND COLDNESS WE PERCEIVE ARE NO MORE IN SNOW, NOR LIGHT AND HEAT IN FIRE,

SPLAT!

HEY!

THAN THE PAIN I FEEL WHEN STUCK BY A NEEDLE IS IN THE NEEDLE.

OR IN THE SNOWBALL!

THESE PERCEPTIONS HAVE NO RESEMBLANCE TO ANYTHING EXISTING IN THE BODIES THEMSELVES.

THE IDEAS OF SECONDARY QUALITIES ARE NOTHING IN BODIES EXCEPT POWERS TO PRODUCE VARIOUS SENSATIONS IN US,

AND DEPEND ON THE PRIMARY QUALITIES OF BULK, FIGURE, TEXTURE, AND MOTION OF PARTS.

THE RED I SEE CORRESPONDS ONLY TO A CORPUSCULAR TEXTURE IN THE ROSE THAT REFLECTS THE PARTICLES OF LIGHT INTO MY EYES IN A CERTAIN WAY.

THIS DISTINCTION AMONG OUR IDEAS IS MEANT TO SHOW HOW THE MECHANICAL PHILOSOPHY'S ACCOUNT OF THE NATURAL WORLD CAN EXPLAIN, AND IS REFLECTED IN, THE CONTENTS OF THE MIND.

OUR SENSORY IDEAS ARE FAIRLY SUPERFICIAL,

AND THEY OFTEN GIVE US ONLY A RELATIVE AND IMPERFECT KNOWLEDGE OF THE DEEPER NATURES OF THINGS.

BUT I'M AFRAID THAT THOSE IDEAS ARE ALL WE HAVE TO GO ON.

LOCKE INSISTS THAT EVEN THE DIVISION OF NATURE'S CREATURES INTO SPECIES IS ONLY A RELATIVE HUMAN CONSTRUCT BASED ON IDEAS OF SENSE EXPERIENCE.

THE BOUNDARIES OF SPECIES, WHEREBY WE SORT THEM,

ARE MADE BY US.

THE "REAL ESSENCES" OF THINGS ARE HIDDEN FROM US.

I CANNOT KNOW THE INTERNAL CORPUSCULAR CONSTITUTION OF A BODY.

AND EVEN IF I COULD, THAT ALONE WOULD NOT HELP ME KNOW WHAT QUALITIES AND POWERS THE BODY HAS —

~?~

AND HOW IT WILL AFFECT SOME OTHER BODY OR MY MIND.

CRASH!

TO CATEGORIZE THINGS AND SORT THEM INTO KINDS WE MUST RELY ON "NOMINAL ESSENCES," ABSTRACT IDEAS PUT TOGETHER BY THE MIND ACCORDING TO EXPERIENCE.

WHAT IS A PIECE OF GOLD BUT SOMETHING THAT ANSWERS TO THE COMPLEX IDEA I HAVE FORMED THAT INCLUDES YELLOW COLOR, A DEGREE OF MALLEABILITY, AND OTHER OBSERVABLE PROPERTIES?

LOCKE, LIKE GASSENDI, DID NOT BELIEVE THAT THE CORPUSCULARIAN THEORY COULD BE CONFIRMED WITH ABSOLUTE CERTAINTY.

OUR KNOWLEDGE IN ALL THESE INQUIRIES REACHES VERY LITTLE FURTHER THAN OUR EXPERIENCE.

AND EXPERIENCE CAN ONLY GO SO FAR.

OUR UNDERSTANDING IS LIMITED TO THE PAUCITY AND IMPERFECTIONS OF THE IDEAS WE HAVE.

WE CANNOT *SEE* CORPUSCLES AND THEIR OPERATIONS — WE CAN ONLY POSTULATE THEIR EXISTENCE.

STILL, THE THEORY FINDS SUPPORT BOTH IN ORDINARY EXPERIENCE AND IN CONTROLLED EXPERIMENT.

I OFFER THE CORPUSCULARIAN HYPOTHESIS SIMPLY AS THAT WHICH IS THOUGHT TO GO FURTHEST

IN AN INTELLIGIBLE EXPLICATION OF THE QUALITIES AND BEHAVIORS OF BODIES.

WHEN I POUND AN ALMOND, ITS WHITE COLOR WILL CHANGE TO A DIRTY ONE, AND ITS SWEET TASTE INTO AN OILY ONE.

BUT WHAT HAVE I ALTERED BESIDES THE ARRANGEMENT OF INSENSIBLE PARTS?

LOCKE PUBLISHED HIS *ESSAY* – AS WELL AS HIS POLITICAL TREATISES – SOON AFTER HIS RETURN TO ENGLAND.

THE WORK WAS OF GREAT INFLUENCE DURING THE ENLIGHTENMENT, PRIMARILY THROUGH FRENCH TRANSLATIONS.

C'EST BON!

TRÈS BIEN!

MAGNIFIQUE!

LEIBNIZ, FOR ONE, WAS IMPRESSED BY WHAT HE READ...

THIS ILLUSTRIOUS ENGLISHMAN HAS PRODUCED ONE OF THE FINEST WORKS OF THE AGE.

...BUT NOT CONVINCED.

TOO BAD HE'S WRONG ABOUT SO MUCH.

HE DECIDED TO COMPOSE A POINT-BY-POINT COMMENTARY ON THE BOOK.

I CALL THEM *NEW ESSAYS ON HUMAN UNDER-STANDING*.

AHEM! PART ONE.

LEIBNIZ TOOK PARTICULAR ISSUE WITH LOCKE'S EMPIRICISM.

OF COURSE, THE SENSES ARE NECESSARY FOR KNOWLEDGE,

BUT THEY ARE NOT SUFFICIENT TO PROVIDE IT ALL.

THE PROBLEM IS THAT SENSE EXPERIENCE ACQUAINTS US ONLY WITH SINGULAR INSTANCES OF THINGS AND EVENTS.

I SEE THAT THIS ROSE IS RED,

THAT ROSE IS RED,

THAT OTHER ROSE IS RED...

WHILE THESE PARTICULARS MAY SUPPORT A GENERAL TRUTH...

LOOK, THIS ROSE IS YELLOW!

SO, ROSES ARE RED... AS FAR AS I CAN TELL.

...THEY CANNOT ESTABLISH THOSE TRUTHS WITH *UNIVERSAL NECESSITY.*

LEIBNIZ INSISTS THAT EXPERIENCE CAN SHOW US WHAT *HAPPENS* TO BE THE CASE AT A PARTICULAR TIME,

I'M STANDING IN A FIELD OF FLOWERS.

I FOUND A YELLOW ROSE!

BUT NOT WHAT *MUST ALWAYS* BE THE CASE OR WHAT *OUGHT* TO BE THE CASE.

ANY TRIANGLE *MUST* HAVE THREE INTERIOR ANGLES THAT ADD UP TO 180 DEGREES.

I SHOULD ACT WITH CHARITY TOWARD MY FELLOW HUMAN BEINGS.

KNOWLEDGE OF THE NECESSARY TRUTHS OF MATHEMATICS, LOGIC, METAPHYSICS, AND ETHICS CANNOT BE EXPLAINED THROUGH EXPERIENCE.

OUR SENSES COULD NEVER TELL US WHAT JUSTICE IS...

OR THAT ONE SHOULD WORSHIP GOD...

OR EVEN THAT TWO PLUS TWO EQUALS FOUR.

A PROOF OF SUCH THINGS THAT REVEALS THEIR NECESSITY CAN ONLY COME FROM INNATE AND INNER PRINCIPLES.

THUS, LEIBNIZ SAYS, LOCKE'S THEORY FAILS ON ITS OWN TERMS —

PSHHHHHH!

THERE ARE CERTAIN THINGS KNOWN BY THE HUMAN MIND THAT CANNOT BE ACCOUNTED FOR BY EXPERIENCE ALONE.

WHY MUST WE ACQUIRE EVERYTHING THROUGH AWARENESS OF OUTER THINGS

AND NOT BE ABLE TO UNEARTH ANYTHING FROM WITHIN OURSELVES?

THIS IS WHAT DISTINGUISHES US FROM THE BEASTS. THEY CAN NEVER FORM NECESSARY PROPOSITIONS.

$E = MC^2$

BUT WE HUMAN BEINGS ARE CAPABLE OF TRUE DEMON-STRATIVE SCIENCE.

HEY, WAIT FOR YOUR OWN CENTURY!

LEIBNIZ BELIEVED THAT LOCKE UNFAIRLY MISCHARACTERIZED THE THEORY OF INNATE IDEAS, SO HE DECIDED TO SET THE ENGLISHMAN STRAIGHT.

IT'S NOT THAT THERE IS ACTUAL KNOWLEDGE OR FULLY FORMED IDEAS CONSCIOUSLY PRESENT IN THE HUMAN MIND AT BIRTH.

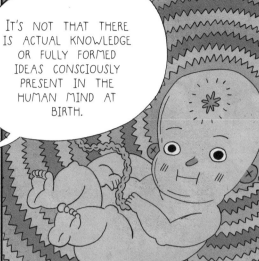

LEIBNIZ PREFERRED TO THINK OF INNATE IDEAS AS INBORN INTELLECTUAL TENDENCIES OR DISPOSITIONS, AS IF THE MIND IS PRE-PROGRAMMED - BY GOD - TO THINK IN CERTAIN WAYS.

WHAT IS *INNATE* IS POTENTIAL KNOWLEDGE OF THESE PRINCIPLES, JUST LIKE THE VEINS OF A BLOCK OF MARBLE OUTLINE A SHAPE WHICH IS ALREADY IN THE MARBLE BEFORE THEY ARE UNCOVERED BY THE SCULPTOR.

THE MIND NEED NOT EVER BECOME CONSCIOUS OF THESE INNATE THINKING TENDENCIES THEMSELVES.

THERE IS NO OBSTACLE TO THERE BEING WITHIN US TRUTHS WHICH HAVE NEVER BEEN

AND WILL NEVER BE THOUGHT ABOUT BY US.

IN HIS *ESSAY*, LOCKE HAD ALREADY REJECTED THIS NOTION AS ABSURD.

IF IT'S THERE IN THE MIND,

WE KNOW IT'S THERE.

WHEN HE FIRST LEARNED OF LEIBNIZ'S CRITICISMS, HE DISMISSED THEM AND THEIR AUTHOR.

EVEN THE LARGEST MINDS HAVE BUT NARROW SWALLOWS.

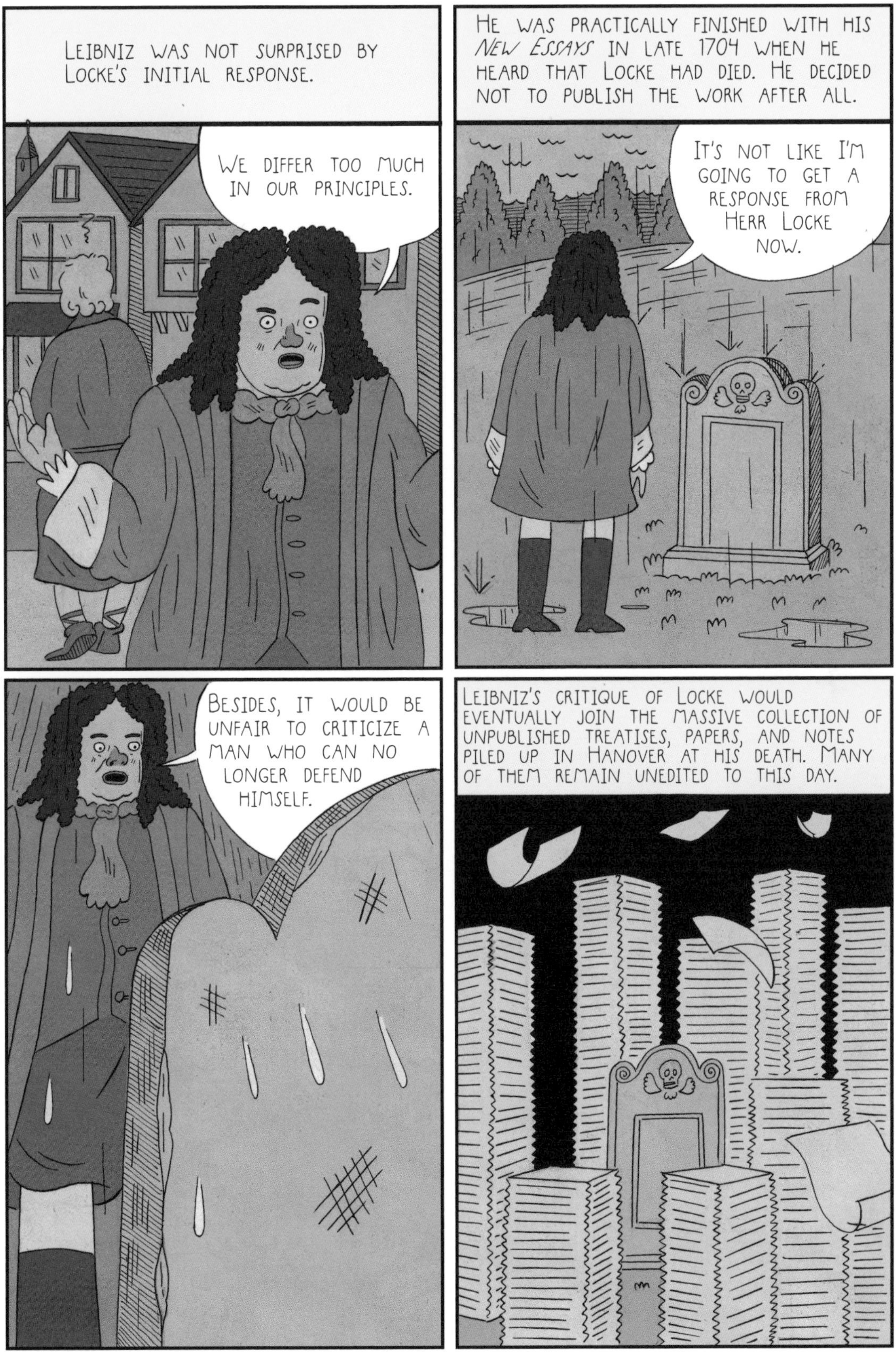
LEIBNIZ WAS NOT SURPRISED BY LOCKE'S INITIAL RESPONSE.
WE DIFFER TOO MUCH IN OUR PRINCIPLES.
HE WAS PRACTICALLY FINISHED WITH HIS NEW ESSAYS IN LATE 1704 WHEN HE HEARD THAT LOCKE HAD DIED. HE DECIDED NOT TO PUBLISH THE WORK AFTER ALL.
IT'S NOT LIKE I'M GOING TO GET A RESPONSE FROM HERR LOCKE NOW.
BESIDES, IT WOULD BE UNFAIR TO CRITICIZE A MAN WHO CAN NO LONGER DEFEND HIMSELF.
LEIBNIZ'S CRITIQUE OF LOCKE WOULD EVENTUALLY JOIN THE MASSIVE COLLECTION OF UNPUBLISHED TREATISES, PAPERS, AND NOTES PILED UP IN HANOVER AT HIS DEATH. MANY OF THEM REMAIN UNEDITED TO THIS DAY.

DESCARTES'S PHILOSOPHY DOMINATED EUROPE THROUGHOUT MOST OF THE 17TH CENTURY. IT WAS ALL THE RAGE IN THE SALONS AND INTELLECTUAL CIRCLES OF PARIS AND OTHER CITIES.

However, problems began to mount.

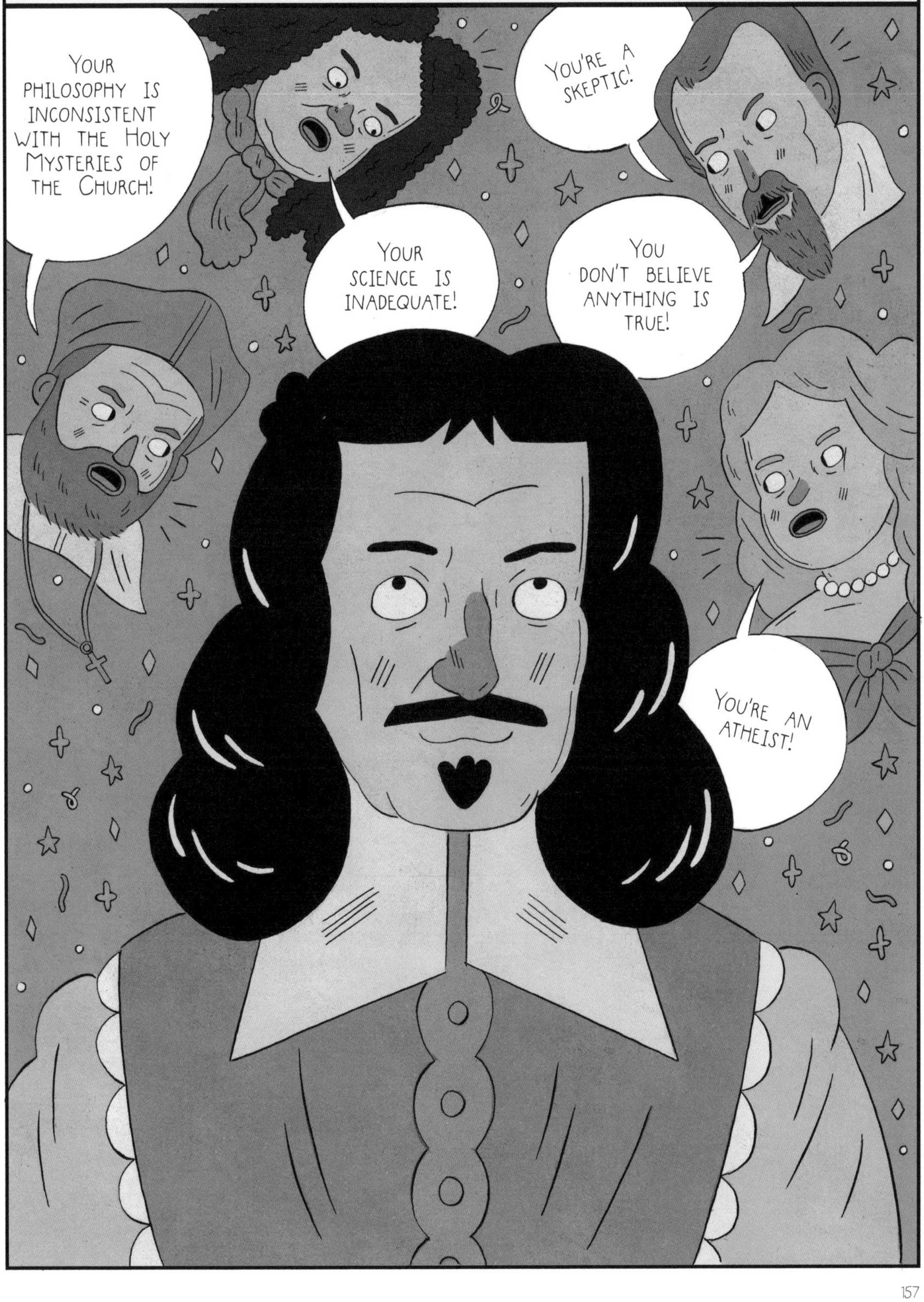
Your philosophy is inconsistent with the Holy Mysteries of the Church!
Your science is inadequate!
You're a skeptic!
You don't believe anything is true!
You're an atheist!

The Catholic hierarchy was bothered by Descartes's reduction of body to mere extension.

If sensible qualities like color, taste, and smell are not really in things,

Then how does the consecrated Eucharistic host still seem like bread?

Natural philosophers did not see how Cartesian physics could provide a proper account of force.

Bodies move, attract, and repel each other — how can you explain that, eh?!

Um...

God?

And some critics suspected that Descartes's professions of religious faith were insincere.

His proofs for God's existence are so bad,

He must have intended them to dissuade people from believing in God!

Descartes's followers defended his philosophy against such attacks.

Don't worry, René. We've got your back!

However, by the end of the century there was a rival philosophy of nature that would, ultimately, prevail.

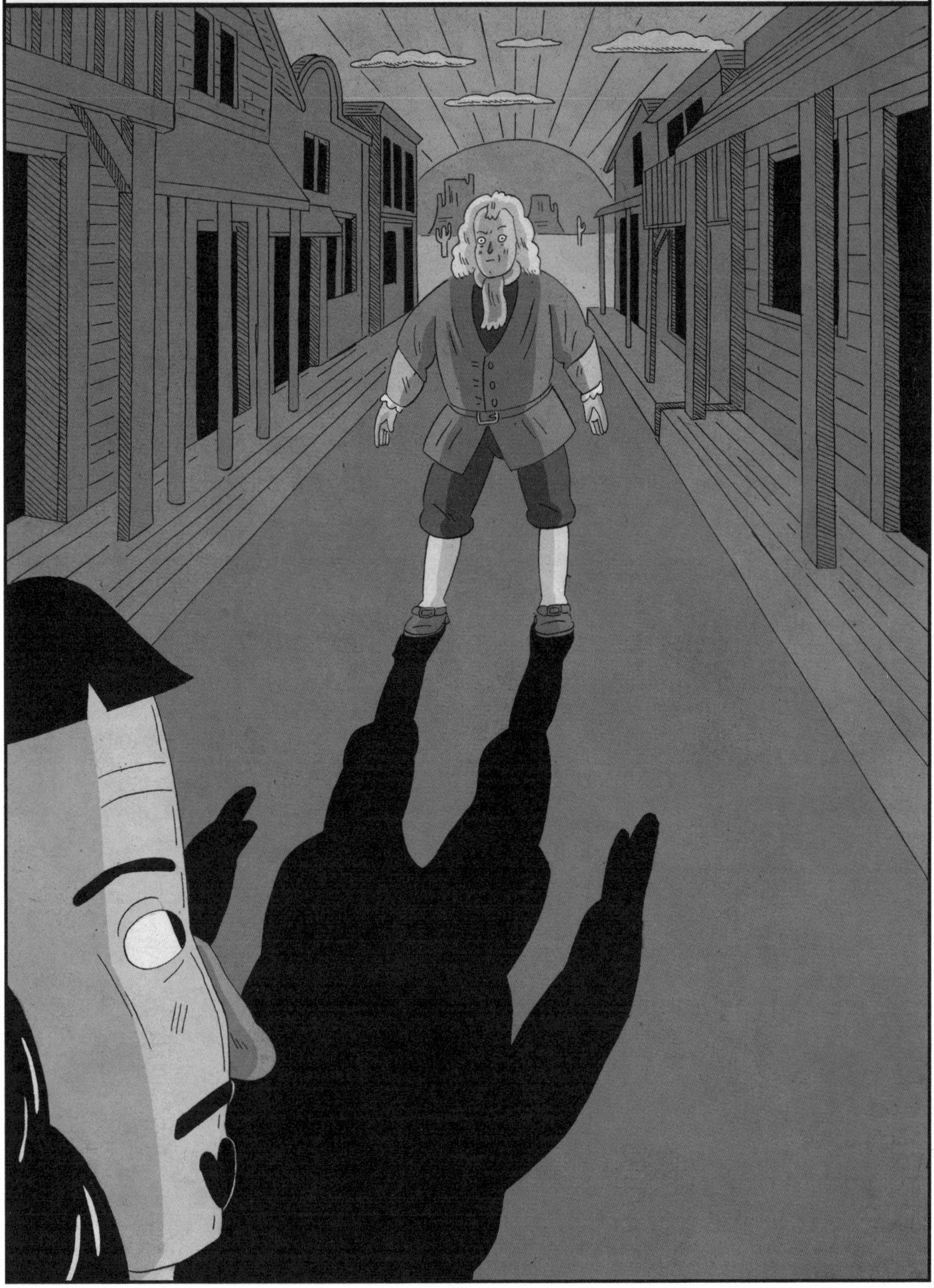

LONDON

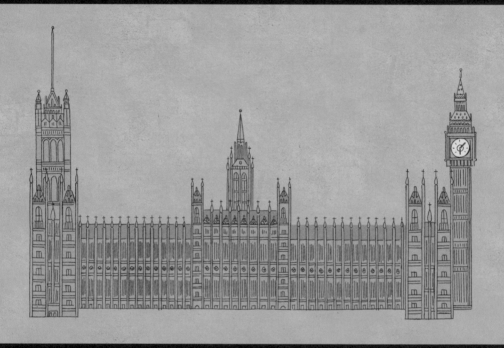

1703

WHEN ISAAC NEWTON WAS ELECTED PRESIDENT OF THE ROYAL SOCIETY IN 1703, IT WAS TESTIMONY TO HIS STATURE AS ENGLAND'S GREATEST NATURAL PHILOSOPHER.

CLAP! CLAP! CLAP! CLAP! CLAP! CLAP!

IN HIS EARLY WORK ON OPTICS, THE CAMBRIDGE SCIENTIST HAD DEMONSTRATED THAT WHITE SUNLIGHT IS IN FACT CONSTITUTED BY DIFFERENTIALLY REFRACTED RAYS OF COLORED LIGHT.

IN 1687, HE PUBLISHED THE MAGISTERIAL:

MATHEMATICAL PRINCIPLES OF NATURAL PHILOSOPHY

ISAAC NEWTON

WITH ITS THREE FUNDAMENTAL LAWS OF MOTION...

EVERY BODY CONTINUES IN ITS STATE OF REST OR UNIFORM MOTION IN A RIGHT LINE UNLESS IT IS COMPELLED TO CHANGE THAT STATE BY FORCES IMPRESSED UPON IT.

THE CHANGE OF MOTION IS PROPORTIONAL TO THE MOTIVE FORCE IMPRESSED AND IS MADE IN THE DIRECTION OF THE RIGHT LINE IN WHICH THAT FORCE IS IMPRESSED.

TO EVERY ACTION THERE IS ALWAYS OPPOSED AN EQUAL REACTION.

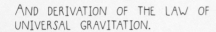

THE FORCE OF GRAVITY IS IN PROPORTION TO THE QUANTITY OF SOLID MATTER IN BODIES AND —

BONK!

AH!

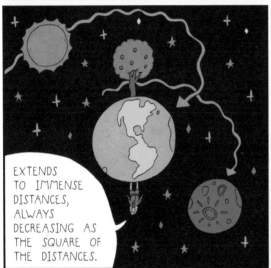

EXTENDS TO IMMENSE DISTANCES, ALWAYS DECREASING AS THE SQUARE OF THE DISTANCES.

NEWTON INSISTED THAT THERE WAS MORE TO THE "PRIMARY" PROPERTIES OF BODIES THAN THOSE THAT DESCARTES, BOYLE, AND LOCKE HAD LISTED.

ALL BODIES ARE HARD, ALL BODIES ARE IMPENETRABLE, ALL BODIES ARE MOBILE,

AND ALL BODIES PERSEVERE IN MOTION BY MEANS OF A FORCE OF INERTIA.

ALTHOUGH NEWTON DENIED THAT GRAVITY, OR HEAVINESS, WAS ALSO SOMETHING ESSENTIAL TO AND INHERENT IN BODIES,

HE INSISTED THAT IT IS A FORCE THAT IS CONSTANTLY ACTING ON ALL BODIES OF THE UNIVERSE.

ALL BODIES EVERYWHERE

ALWAYS GRAVITATE TOWARD ONE ANOTHER.

THE SAME FORCE THAT KEEPS THE PLANETS AND COMETS IN ORBIT AROUND THE SUN, AND THE MOON IN ORBIT AROUND THE EARTH...

MAKES AN APPLE FALL TO THE GROUND.

AGAIN? REALLY?

SOMETIMES NEWTON SPOKE OF GRAVITY AS IF IT WERE A MYSTERIOUS POWER THAT OPERATED ACROSS EMPTY SPACE WITHOUT ANY INTERVENING MECHANISM.

HE INSISTED, THOUGH, THAT GRAVITY (OR MAGNETISM OR ELECTRICITY) IS NOT A HIDDEN "OCCULT QUALITY."

IT IS PLAIN FROM THE PHENOMENA THAT SUCH A POWER DOES ACTUALLY EXIST.

AND HE DID NOT REGARD TRUE ACTION AT A DISTANCE AS A REAL POSSIBILITY.

IT IS INCONCEIVABLE THAT INANIMATE, BRUTE MATTER

SHOULD OPERATE UPON AND AFFECT OTHER MATTER WITHOUT MUTUAL CONTACT.

THERE HAD TO BE SOMETHING UNOBSERVABLE THAT, ACTING ON VISIBLE BODIES, EXPLAINED THEIR MUTUAL ATTRACTION.

ONE BODY CANNOT ACT UPON ANOTHER AT A DISTANCE THROUGH A VACUUM WITHOUT THE MEDIATION OF SOMETHING ELSE, WHETHER MATERIAL OR IMMATERIAL.

ON OCCASION HE WAS WILLING TO SPECULATE ON WHAT MIGHT BE THE UNDERLYING CAUSE OF GRAVITATIONAL ATTRACTION.

THERE'S GOTTA BE SOMETHING THERE.

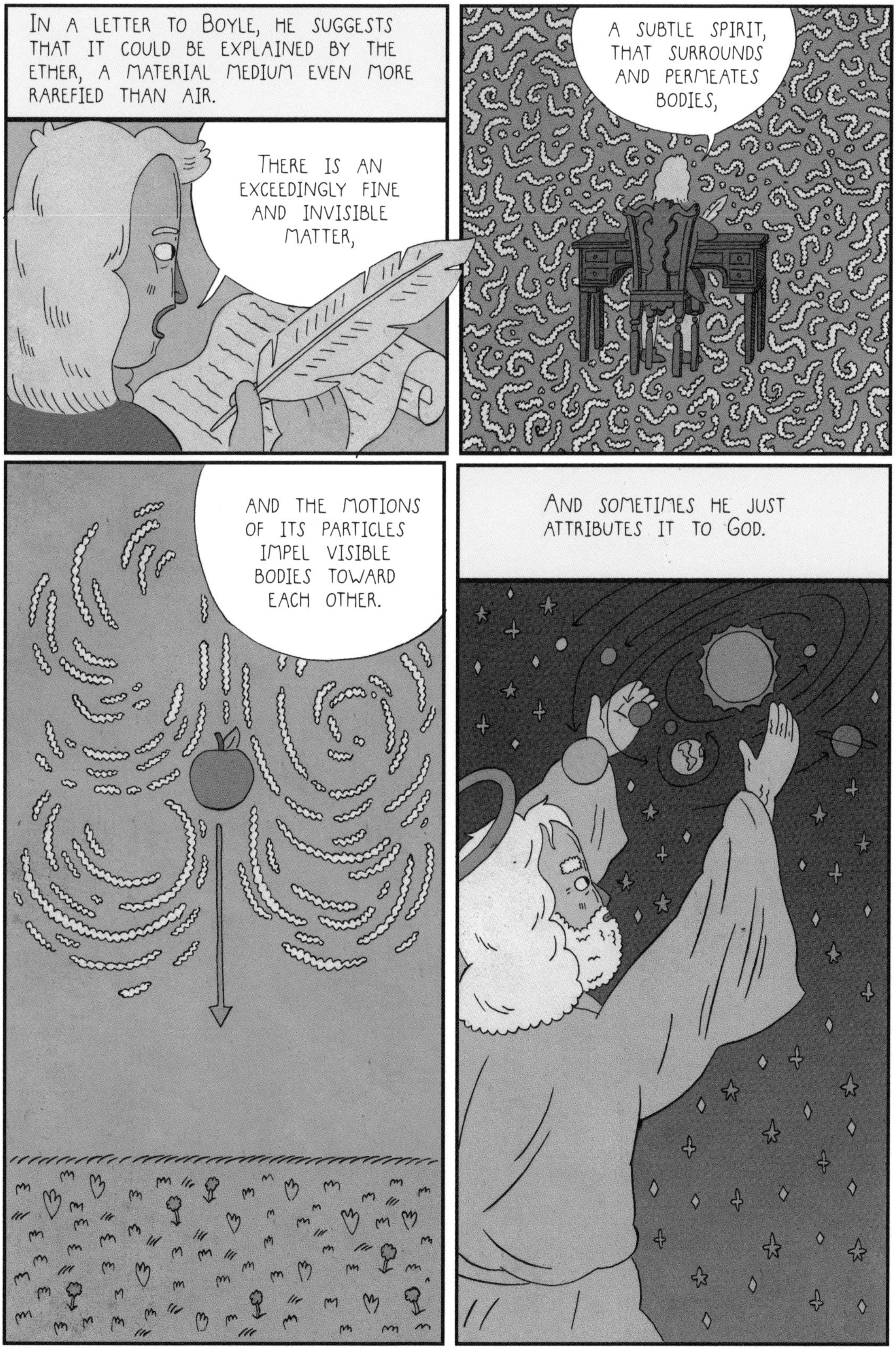
IN A LETTER TO BOYLE, HE SUGGESTS THAT IT COULD BE EXPLAINED BY THE ETHER, A MATERIAL MEDIUM EVEN MORE RAREFIED THAN AIR.
THERE IS AN EXCEEDINGLY FINE AND INVISIBLE MATTER,
A SUBTLE SPIRIT, THAT SURROUNDS AND PERMEATES BODIES,
AND THE MOTIONS OF ITS PARTICLES IMPEL VISIBLE BODIES TOWARD EACH OTHER.
AND SOMETIMES HE JUST ATTRIBUTES IT TO GOD.

BUT NEWTON'S PREFERRED STANCE WAS AGNOSTICISM.

HOW THE ATTRACTIONS OF GRAVITY,

MAGNETISM,

AND ELECTRICITY MAY BE PERFORMED,

I DO NOT KNOW.

HE DID NOT WANT TO ENGAGE IN "HYPOTHESIZING" ABOUT HIDDEN CAUSES.

HYPOTHESES NON FINGO. *

*I DO NOT INVENT HYPOTHESES.

NEWTON WAS RELUCTANT TO OFFER AN EXPLANATION OF *WHY* BODIES ATTRACT EACH OTHER BY POSTULATING SOME UNVERIFIABLE CAUSAL MECHANISM.

LET DESCARTES AND LEIBNIZ PLAY THAT GAME. I HAVE BETTER THINGS TO DO.

WHAT? YOU DON'T LIKE MY VORTICES?

NO, I DON'T. THERE IS NO EMPIRICAL EVIDENCE TO SUPPORT SUCH METAPHYSICAL SPECULATIONS.

WHATEVER IS NOT DEDUCED FROM THE PHENOMENA MUST BE CALLED A HYPOTHESIS, AND SUCH SPECULATIONS, WHETHER METAPHYSICAL OR PHYSICAL,

OR BASED ON OCCULT QUALITIES, HAVE NO PLACE IN EXPERIMENTAL PHILOSOPHY.

NEWTON PREFERRED TO LIMIT HIMSELF TO WHAT CAN BE KNOWN ABOUT THE FORCES OF NATURE AS "MANIFEST QUALITIES," WITHOUT DELVING INTO UNSEEN CAUSES.

$$F_G = G \frac{m_1 \, m_2}{}$$

I CONSIDER THESE FORCES NOT FROM A PHYSICAL BUT ONLY FROM A MATHEMATICAL POINT OF VIEW.

BUT MY GOOD MAN, YOU HAVE BIGGER PROBLEMS THAN UNWARRANTED METAPHYSICAL SPECULATIONS ABOUT CAUSES.

BY EQUATING MATTER WITH EXTENSION, DESCARTES MADE BODY IDENTICAL TO SPACE.

THE UNIVERSE IS A PLENUM.

BODY IS EVERYWHERE.

For Descartes, there is no space independent of bodies in which they exist and move.

Motion is simply the transference of a body

From the vicinity of those bodies immediately contiguous with it and considered as at rest,

Into the vicinity of some other bodies.

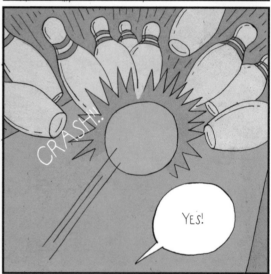

CRASH!

Yes!

Leibniz agreed with Descartes that space is something merely relative.

Space consists only in the relations between bodies.

Newton regarded this position as both absurd in itself and contrary to observation.

If Descartes is right, then no body's motion can be said to be more true, absolute, and proper than another's.

ACCORDING TO NEWTON, SOME MOTIONS ARE REAL,

WHILE OTHERS ARE ONLY APPARENT.

AND ONLY AN ABSOLUTE CONCEPTION OF SPACE WOULD ALLOW ONE TO SAY THAT ONE BODY REALLY IS IN MOTION

AND ANOTHER BODY REALLY AT REST.

SPACE EXTENDS INFINITELY IN ALL DIRECTIONS.

IT EXISTS INDEPENDENT OF WHATEVER IS CONTAINED IN IT.

SPACES ARE NOT THE VERY BODIES THEMSELVES, BUT IT IS WHERE BODIES EXIST AND MOVE.

THUS THERE ARE ABSOLUTE PLACES IN SPACE,

AND IT IS ONLY CHANGE OF POSITION FROM ONE ABSOLUTE PLACE TO ANOTHER THAT IS TRUE AND ABSOLUTE MOTION.

LEIBNIZ WAS ABLE TO ACCOMMODATE THE REALITY OF MOTION *WITHOUT* ABSOLUTE SPACE

BY PLACING METAPHYSICAL AND DYNAMIC FORCES *IN* BODIES.

DESCARTES, WHO ACKNOWLEDGED ONLY PASSIVE EXTENSION IN BODIES,

WAS NOT.

NEWTON, TOO, ALLOWED THAT A BODY IS *REALLY* IN MOTION IF THERE IS A FORCE OPERATING ON IT.

THE CAUSES WHICH DISTINGUISH TRUE MOTIONS FROM MERELY RELATIVE MOTIONS

ARE THE FORCES IMPRESSED UPON BODIES TO GENERATE MOTION.

IN MOTION

AT REST

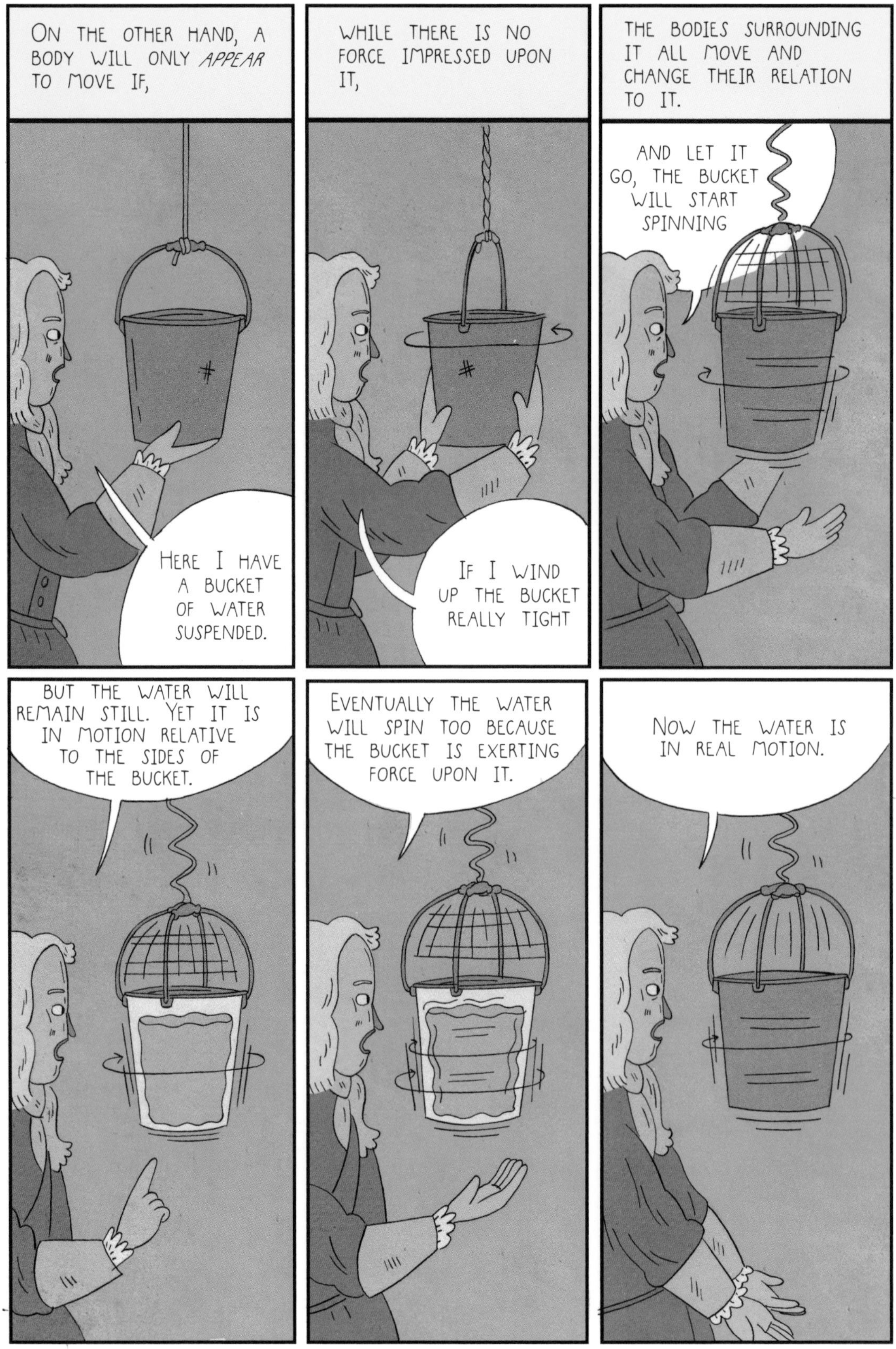
ON THE OTHER HAND, A BODY WILL ONLY APPEAR TO MOVE IF,
HERE I HAVE A BUCKET OF WATER SUSPENDED.
WHILE THERE IS NO FORCE IMPRESSED UPON IT,
IF I WIND UP THE BUCKET REALLY TIGHT
THE BODIES SURROUNDING IT ALL MOVE AND CHANGE THEIR RELATION TO IT.
AND LET IT GO, THE BUCKET WILL START SPINNING
BUT THE WATER WILL REMAIN STILL. YET IT IS IN MOTION RELATIVE TO THE SIDES OF THE BUCKET.
EVENTUALLY THE WATER WILL SPIN TOO BECAUSE THE BUCKET IS EXERTING FORCE UPON IT.
NOW THE WATER IS IN REAL MOTION.

THE COSMOS THAT NEWTON DESCRIBED WITH REAL FORCES OPERATING ON BODIES IN ABSOLUTE SPACE WAS A VERY DIFFERENT PLACE FROM WHAT DESCARTES HAD PROPOSED HALF A CENTURY EARLIER.

EPILOGUE: GENEVA

1755

THE 18TH-CENTURY FRENCH *PHILOSOPHE* FRANCOIS-MARIE AVOUET, BETTER KNOWN BY HIS PEN-NAME, "VOLTAIRE,"

SPENT A GOOD DEAL OF TIME CONSIDERING THE PHILOSOPHICAL LEGACIES OF THE PREVIOUS CENTURY.

HIS SATIRE *CANDIDE* POKED FUN AT LEIBNIZ'S OPTIMISTIC THEODICY.

IS THIS NOT OBVIOUSLY THE BEST OF ALL POSSIBLE WORLDS?

HE HAD NOTHING BUT SCORN FOR PASCAL'S CHRISTIAN PIETY.

BUT IT WAS THE CONTRAST BETWEEN DESCARTES AND NEWTON THAT REALLY CAUGHT HIS ATTENTION.

A FRENCHMAN WHO ARRIVES IN LONDON WILL FIND PHILOSOPHY, LIKE EVERYTHING ELSE, VERY MUCH CHANGED THERE.

HAVING LEFT A WORLD THAT IS A PLENUM, HE NOW FINDS IT A VACUUM.

AT PARIS THE UNIVERSE IS SEEN TO BE COMPOSED OF VORTICES OF SUBTLE MATTER,

BUT NOTHING LIKE THIS IS SEEN IN LONDON.

THE VERY ESSENCE OF THINGS IS TOTALLY CHANGED.

VOLTAIRE RESPECTED BOTH DESCARTES AND NEWTON...

BUT HE KNEW THAT THE ENGLISHMAN'S PHILOSOPHY HAD WON THE DAY.

IT MUST BE CONFESSED THAT THESE TWO GREAT MEN DIFFERED VERY MUCH IN CONDUCT, IN FORTUNE,

AND IN PHILOSOPHY.

WE MAY ADMIRE SIR ISAAC NEWTON,

BUT WE MUST NOT CENSURE DESCARTES.

THE OPINION THAT GENERALLY PREVAILS IN ENGLAND WITH REGARD TO THESE NEW PHILOSOPHERS IS THAT DESCARTES WAS A DREAMER,

AND NEWTON A SAGE.

WHAT CAUSED VOLTAIRE THE MOST DISMAY, HOWEVER, WERE THE RELIGIOUS FORCES THAT TRIED - IN THE END, UNSUCCESSFULLY - TO SMOTHER PHILOSOPHY AND HALT THE PROGRESS OF KNOWLEDGE.

WHEN ONE CONSIDERS THAT NEWTON, LOCKE, AND LEIBNIZ WOULD HAVE BEEN PERSECUTED IN FRANCE,

IMPRISONED IN ROME,

AND BURNED IN LISBON, WHAT ARE WE TO THINK OF HUMAN REASON?

THEY WHO PUT GALILEO BEFORE THE INQUISITION WERE WRONG,

AND EVERY INQUISITOR OUGHT TO BLUSH, FROM THE BOTTOM OF HIS SOUL, AT THE SIGHT OF THE SPHERE OF COPERNICUS.

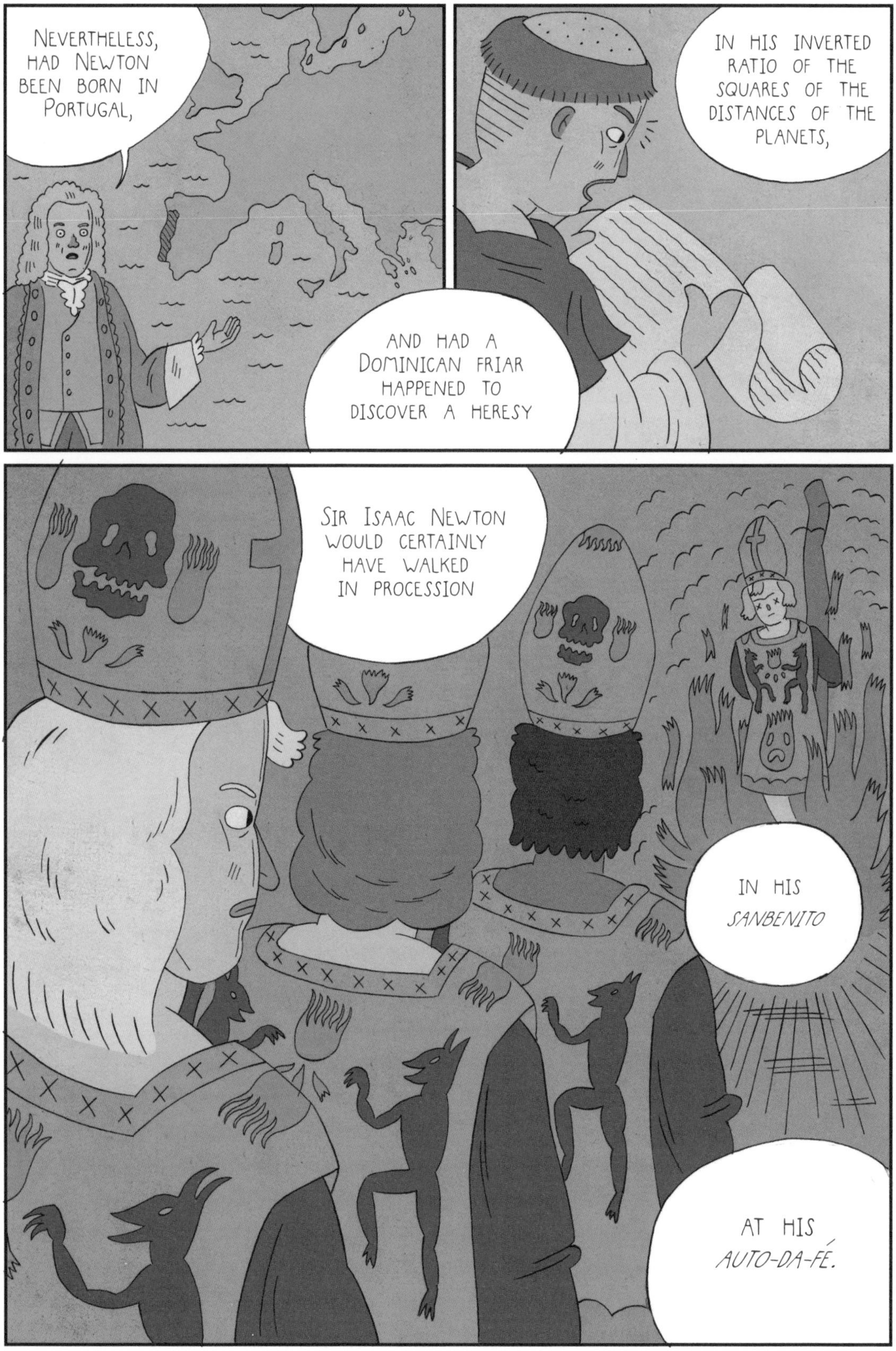
NEVERTHELESS, HAD NEWTON BEEN BORN IN PORTUGAL,
IN HIS INVERTED RATIO OF THE SQUARES OF THE DISTANCES OF THE PLANETS,
AND HAD A DOMINICAN FRIAR HAPPENED TO DISCOVER A HERESY
SIR ISAAC NEWTON WOULD CERTAINLY HAVE WALKED IN PROCESSION
IN HIS *SANBENITO*
AT HIS *AUTO-DA-FÉ*.

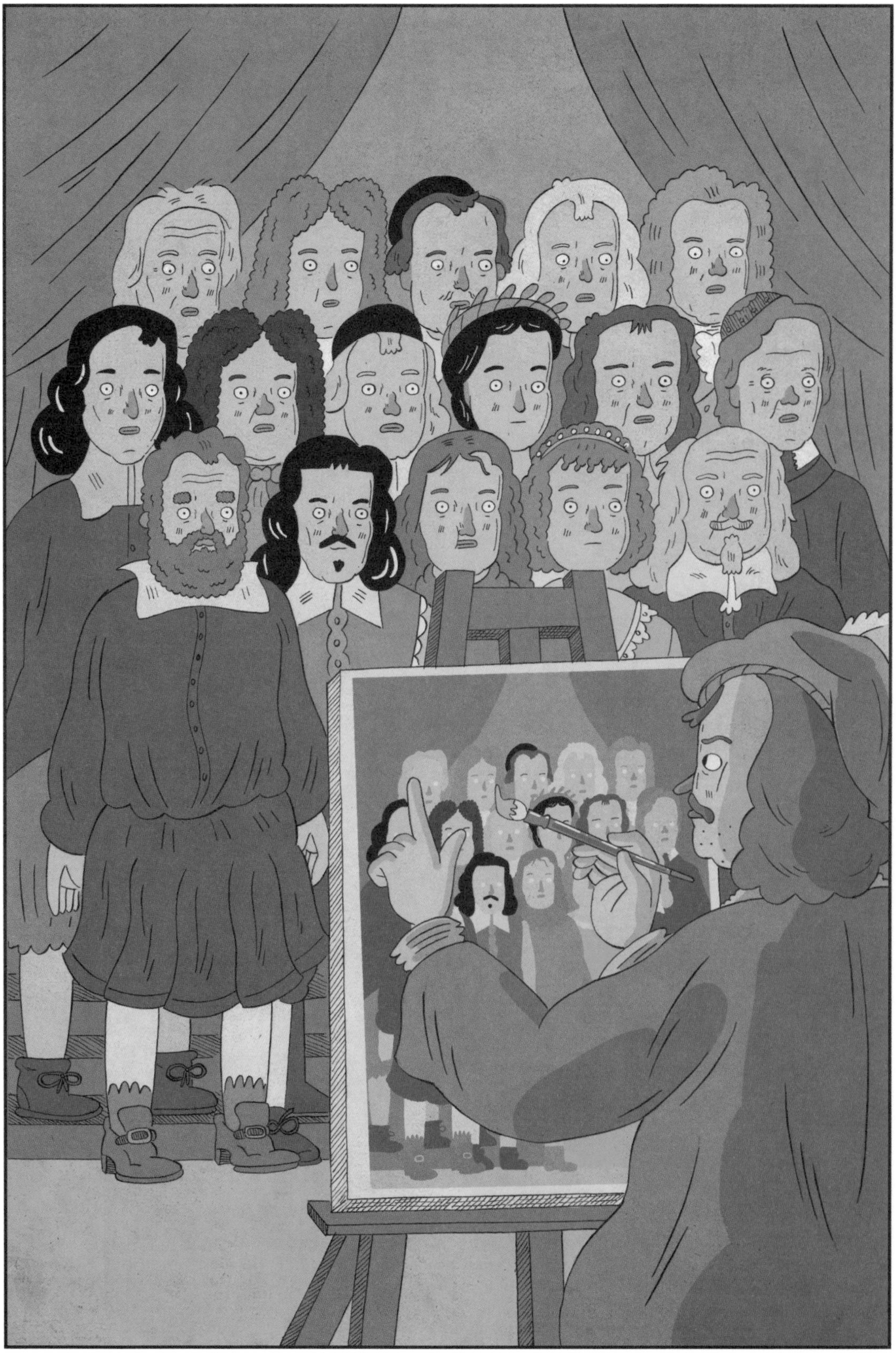

DRAMATIS PERSONAE

(PART ONE)

ANTOINE ARNAULD
(B. PARIS, 1612; D. LIÈGE, FLANDERS, 1694)

CATHOLIC PRIEST, THEOLOGIAN, AND PHILOSOPHER. HIS MAIN PHILOSOPHICAL WRITINGS INCLUDE THE "FOURTH SET OF OBJECTIONS" TO DESCARTES'S *MEDITATIONS* (1641), *ON TRUE AND FALSE IDEAS* (1683), AND HIS CORRESPONDENCES WITH MALEBRANCHE AND LEIBNIZ.

FRANCIS BACON
(B. 1561, LONDON; D. HIGHGATE, 1626)

ENGLISH NATURAL PHILOSOPHER, LAWYER, STATESMAN. PUBLISHED *THE ADVANCEMENT OF LEARNING* IN 1605, AND *NOVUM ORGANUM* (*NEW ORGANUM*), PART OF THE *INSTAURATIO MAGNA* (*THE GREAT RESTORATION*), IN 1620.

ROBERT BOYLE
(B. LISMORE, IRELAND, 1627; D. LONDON, 1691)

NATURAL PHILOSOPHER. HIS PUBLISHED WORKS INCLUDE *NEW EXPERIMENTS PHYSICO-MECHANICALL, TOUCHING THE SPRING OF THE AIR* (1660), *THE SCEPTICAL CHYMIST* (1661), AND *ORIGINE OF FORMES AND QUALITIES* (1666).

GIORDANO BRUNO
(B. NOLA, ITALY, 1548; D. ROME 1600)

DOMINICAN FRIAR AND ITALIAN PHILOSOPHER AND THEOLOGIAN. AMONG HIS MANY WORKS ARE *THE ART OF MEMORY* (1582), *THE ASH WEDNESDAY SUPPER* (1584), AND *ON THE INFINITE UNIVERSE AND WORLDS* (1584).

ANNE CONWAY
(B. LONDON, 1631; D. WARWICKSHIRE, 1679)

ENGLISH PHILOSOPHER AND THEOLOGIAN. SHE IS THE AUTHOR OF *THE PRINCIPLES OF THE MOST ANCIENT AND MODERN PHILOSOPHY* (1690).

RENÉ DESCARTES
(B. LA HAYE, FRANCE, 1596; D. STOCKHOLM, 1650)

FRENCH PHILOSOPHER AND MATHEMATICIAN. HIS WORKS INCLUDE *THE WORLD* (1628-1633, UNPUBLISHED IN HIS LIFETIME), *DISCOURSE ON METHOD* (WITH ACCOMPANYING ESSAYS ON OPTICS, METEOROLOGY, AND GEOMETRY, 1637), *MEDITATIONS ON FIRST PHILOSOPHY* (1641), *PRINCIPLES OF PHILOSOPHY* (1644), AND *THE PASSIONS OF THE SOUL* (1649).

DRAMATIS PERSONAE

(PART TWO)

ELISABETH OF BOHEMIA (PRINCESS PALATINE)
(B. HEIDELBERG, 1618; D. HERFORD, ENGLAND, 1680)

SHE ENGAGED IN PHILOSOPHICALLY RICH CORRESPONDENCE WITH DESCARTES, LEIBNIZ, MALEBRANCHE, AND OTHERS.

GALILEO GALILEI
(B. PISA, 1564; D. FLORENCE, 1642)

ITALIAN NATURAL PHILOSOPHER. HIS MAJOR WORKS ARE *THE STARRY MESSENGER* (1610), *THE ASSAYER* (1623), *DIALOGUE ON THE TWO CHIEF WORLD SYSTEMS* (1632), AND *DISCOURSES AND MATHEMATICAL DEMONSTRATIONS OF TWO NEW SCIENCES* (1638).

PIERRE GASSENDI
(B. CHAMPTERCIER, PROVENCE, 1592; D. PARIS 1655)

FRENCH PHILOSOPHER AND THEOLOGIAN. HE IS THE AUTHOR OF THE "FIFTH SET OF OBJECTIONS" TO DESCARTES'S *MEDITATIONS* (1641), FOLLOWED BY THE ANTI-CARTESIAN *METAPHYSICAL DISQUISITION* (1644) AND THE *SYNTAGMA PHILOSOPHICUM* (1658), AMONG OTHER WRITINGS.

THOMAS HOBBES
(B. MALMESBURY, WILTSHIRE, 1588; D. DERBYSHIRE, 1679)

ENGLISH PHILOSOPHER AND MATHEMATICIAN. HIS WORKS INCLUDE THE "THIRD SET OF OBJECTIONS" TO DESCARTES'S *MEDITATIONS* (1641); THE *ELEMENTS OF PHILOSOPHY*, COMPRISED OF THREE TREATISES: *ON THE CITIZEN* (1642), *ON BODY* (1656), AND *ON MAN* (1658); AND *LEVIATHAN* (1651).

GOTTFRIED WILHELM LEIBNIZ
(B. LEIPZIG, 1646; D. HANOVER, 1716)

GERMAN PHILOSOPHER, THEOLOGIAN, MATHEMATICIAN, HISTORIAN, ETC. HIS VOLUMINOUS WRITINGS INCLUDE *DISCOURSE ON METAPHYSICS* (1686, UNPUBLISHED IN HIS LIFETIME); *NEW SYSTEM OF NATURE* (1695); *NEW ESSAYS ON HUMAN UNDERSTANDING* (1704, UNPUBLISHED IN HIS LIFETIME); *THEODICY* (1710); AND *PRINCIPLES OF NATURE AND OF GRACE* AND *MONADOLOGY* (BOTH 1714, UNPUBLISHED IN HIS LIFETIME), ALONG WITH IMPORTANT CORRESPONDENCE WITH AN ENORMOUS NUMBER OF PEOPLE, INCLUDING SPINOZA, ARNAULD, AND MALEBRANCHE.

JOHN LOCKE
(B. SOMERSET, 1632; D. ESSEX, 1704)

ENGLISH PHILOSOPHER AND PHYSICIAN. HIS MOST IMPORTANT PHILOSOPHICAL WRITINGS ARE *AN ESSAY CONCERNING HUMAN UNDERSTANDING* (1690), *TWO TREATISES ON GOVERNMENT* (1690), *SOME THOUGHTS CONCERNING EDUCATION* (1695), AND SEVERAL "LETTERS" ON TOLERATION.

DRAMATIS PERSONAE

(PART THREE)

NICOLAS MALEBRANCHE
(B. PARIS, 1638; D. PARIS, 1715)

FRENCH THEOLOGIAN AND PHILOSOPHER AND CATHOLIC PRIEST (ORATORY). HE IS THE AUTHOR OF *THE SEARCH AFTER TRUTH* (1674-75), *TREATISE ON NATURE AND GRACE* (1680), *DIALOGUES ON METAPHYSICS AND RELIGION* (1688), AND PHILOSOPHICAL CORRESPONDENCE WITH ARNAULD, LEIBNIZ, AND MANY OTHERS.

HENRY MORE
(B. GRANTHAM, LINCOLNSHIRE, 1614; D. CAMBRIDGE, 1687)

ENGLISH PHILOSOPHER AND THEOLOGIAN. HIS MAJOR WORKS INCLUDE *PSYCHODIA PLATONICA; OR, A PLATONICALL SONG OF THE SOUL* (1642), *AN ANTIDOTE AGAINST ATHEISME* (1653), AND *THE IMMORTALITY OF THE SOUL* (1659).

SIR ISAAC NEWTON
(B. WOOLSTHORPE, LINCOLNSHIRE, 1643; D. LONDON, 1727)

ENGLISH NATURAL PHILOSOPHER AND MATHEMATICIAN. AMONG HIS MOST IMPORTANT PHILOSOPHICAL WRITINGS ARE "NEW THEORY OF LIGHT AND COLORS" (1672), *MATHEMATICAL PRINCIPLES OF NATURAL PHILOSOPHY* (1687), AND *OPTICKS* (1704).

BLAISE PASCAL
(B. CLERMONT-FERRAND, 1623; D. PARIS, 1662)

FRENCH MATHEMATICIAN, NATURAL PHILOSOPHER, AND RELIGIOUS WRITER. HIS WORKS INCLUDE *TREATISE ON THE VACUUM* (1651), *PROVINCIAL LETTERS* (1656-57), AND THE *PENSÉES* (BEGUN IN 1658, NOT PUBLISHED UNTIL 1670).

BENTO (BENEDICTUS) SPINOZA
(B. AMSTERDAM, 1632; D. THE HAGUE, 1677)

DUTCH PHILOSOPHER OF PORTUGUESE-JEWISH ANCESTRY. HIS MAJOR WORKS ARE *TREATISE ON THE EMENDATION OF THE INTELLECT* (UNPUBLISHED IN HIS LIFETIME), *SHORT TREATISE ON GOD, MAN, AND HIS WELL-BEING* (UNPUBLISHED IN HIS LIFETIME), *DESCARTES'S PRINCIPLES OF PHILOSOPHY AND METAPHYSICAL THOUGHTS* (1663), *ETHICS* (COMPOSED CA. 1662-1676, PUBLISHED POSTHUMOUSLY IN 1677), *THEOLOGICAL-POLITICAL TREATISE* (1670), AND *POLITICAL TREATISE* (UNFINISHED).

VOLTAIRE
(FRANCOIS-MARIE AVOUET)
(B. PARIS, 1694; D. PARIS, 1778)

FRENCH WRITER. HIS WORKS INCLUDE *PHILOSOPHICAL LETTERS CONCERNING THE ENGLISH NATION* (1754) AND *CANDIDE* (1759), AS WELL AS MANY HISTORICAL WRITINGS, TREATISES ON RELIGION, PLAYS, AND LETTERS.

Acknowledgments

It goes without saying that a book like this depends on the generosity of friends and colleagues – both for their encouragement and for their brutally honest feedback. Our thanks to Callan Berry, Daniel Garber, Andrew Janiak, Debra Nails, Don Rutherford, Larry Shapiro, Elliott Sober, and Norma Sober for reading, re-reading, and proofreading, for telling us what works and what doesn't, and for other help along the way.

Then there are family and loved ones whose patience, humor, advice, and insight have sustained us well beyond the confines of this project: Jane Bernstein (wife of Steven, mother of Ben – the cover design was her idea), Rose Nadler (daughter of Steven and Jane, sister of Ben), and Nette Oot.

Steven would like to express his gratitude to the American Academy in Rome and its directors Chris Celenza and Kim Bowles, for the invitation to be a Scholar-in-Residence in the spring of 2014. Some of the writing of the text took place during that glorious month.

And finally, a special thanks to Rob Tempio at Princeton University Press. We could not have done it without his enthusiasm and support. Indispensible help was also provided by the production team at the Press: Mark Bellis, Dimitri Karetnikov, and Jessica Massabrook.